Alexander Clinton

Advantages and Necessity of Frequent Communion

Asserted and Proved

Alexander Clinton

Advantages and Necessity of Frequent Communion
Asserted and Proved

ISBN/EAN: 9783744659642

Printed in Europe, USA, Canada, Australia, Japan

Cover: Foto ©ninafisch / pixelio.de

More available books at **www.hansebooks.com**

ADVANTAGES
—AND—
NECESSITY
—OF—
FREQUENT COMMUNION

ASSERTED AND PROVED,

FROM

SCRIPTURE, AUTHORITY

—AND—

TRADITION.

BY A. C.

"Except you eat the Flesh of the Son of Man, and drink His Blood, you shall not have Life in you.—John vi. 54.

L. F. KILROY,
DETROIT, MICH.
1883.

INTRODUCTION.

The present volume is a reprint of an old work published in London, England, in the year 1780. Treating as it does, in an exhaustive manner, of one of the most practically important points in the spiritual life, it cannot but be highly beneficial to souls anxious for salvation and perfection. As we have unfortunately, few works in English on frequent communion, it was thought much good would be done by placing within reach of all, a book that otherwise could not be had, by reason of its being, apparently at least, out of print.

Communion is the soul's life. "The bread that I will give you, "says Christ," is my flesh for the life of the world." The better, therefore, the nature of this heavenly food is understood, the more Christ's designs regarding it are known, the more certainly will it produce the effects intended by its divine donor. Christ's designs regarding it can be gathered from His words in reference to it, from the utterances of His Apostles, from the practices of the early Christians, from the teaching of the Fathers, who are witnesses to the Church's traditions in their respective ages, from the decisions of councils, general and particular, and from the authoritative utterances of the sovereign Pontiffs. These are all placed before the reader in the work now offered to the faithful, and he is then left to draw his own conclusions regarding the particular kind of homage he should pay to his hidden God in the Sacrament of His love. He cannot fail to see that Christ left us Himself in holy communion to be eaten, to be eaten frequently, and that so long as we refuse Him such homage, we deny Him that which, of all others, He is the most anxious to receive. If the consoling and salutary teaching contained in this valuable old book will only have the effect of exciting souls to a greater love for frequent communion, if it will only lead them to a more frequent use of this great sacrament the labor bestowed on its reproduction will be amply repaid.

Feast of the Presentation of the Blessed Virgin.
Detroit Mich. 1883.

ON FREQUENT COMMUNION.

CHAPTER I.

THE PRETENDED RESPECT FOR THE BLESSED EUCHARIST, WHICH WITHDRAWS THE FAITHFUL FROM FREQUENT COMMUNION, IS ERRONEOUS AND DANGEROUS.

THE Holy Ghost warns us to avoid giving ear to every report, or credit to every appearance of rectitude and virtue,* because deceit is often palliated with a cloak of justice, and error lies frequently masked under the features of truth. Most, if not all religious matters, have been at times misunderstood and traduced, and frequent communion, perhaps, as much as any other religious duty, has been strangely misconstrued. At this present time, thousands among the faithful labor under dangerous mistakes relative to this important question; even some of the pastors of the church of Christ, either vainly intimidated by certain fallacious reasonings on church discipline,

---

* There is a way which seemeth just to a man, but the ends thereof lead to death.—[Prov. xiv. 2.

or led away by a relish for rigorism, reluctantly teach and encourage frequent communion; whilst others, less excusable, from an adoption of erroneous principles, positively oppose and condemn it; but what is no less remarkable than surprising, the loosest christians and the greatest sinners join in opinion with the rigorists, and unanimously applaud that false respect which with-holds from the sacred table, even at those times when a strict precept for communion is actually in force, and directly urging.

True respect, true humility, in the opinion of St. Gregory, consists in a docile submission to, and a ready compliance with what lawful authority enjoins as an useful help to salvation; from whence the scholastic Doctor St. Thomas concludes, that there can be no real religion or humility in him, who, in opposition to the law of Christ, or of His church, and I venture to add in opposition to the opinion of every prudent and discreet director,* abstains from communion.

The expression of St. Cyril, of Alexandria, on this subject is extremely forcible, and claims great

---

*Ideo non potest esse laudabilis humilitas, si contra præceptum Christi & Ecclesiæ aliquis omnino a communione abstineat. D Thom. 3. p. q. 80. ar. 11 ad. 1.

attention: "If we would attain life everlasting, if we would possess the Author of immortality, let us readily and willingly receive the Eucharist; and let us be greatly on our guard lest the devil should ensnare us in a damnable religion, through a pretended motive of respect for this sacrament."*
From these words it evidently appears, that this delusive respect and mistaken religion, is an old stratagem, which this holy father terms a damnable religion, of which he assigns the devil as the author, and styles it as an infernal artifice, against which we should greatly be guarded.

The above sentence the Church has inserted into the office of the blessed sacrament, on the last day of the Octave, that all bishops and priests, in every part of the world, and in every age, might join this holy father in publishing to the faithful, that the religion which indiscriminately dissuades and withdraws them from a participation of the Eucharist, is dangerous, hurtful and diabolical.

And, in fact, nothing can be more suitable to the evil designs and malicious purposes of the common enemy to man, than this false religion, for the

---

* Nos vero si vitam æternam consequi volumus, si largitorem immortalitatis habere in nobis desideramus, ad recipiendam benedictionem libenter concurramus; caveamusque, ne loco laquei, damnosam religionem diabolus nobis prætendat, S. Cyril, l. 4. in Joan. c. 17.

Eucharist is of all the sacraments the most salutary and beneficial to Christian people, it is the very source of all heavenly graces; it consequently must follow, that the longer we abstain from it the fewer of these graces we shall ordinarily obtain; tepidity will presently succeed to our primitive fervor, and the vigor of our souls will soon sink into a languid state of remissness.

The man who should abstain from all corporal nourishment would inevitably perish, were there no other cause for his dissolution; in like manner the Christian, who for any length of time refrains from this heavenly food, must droop in spirit, and slacken in the path of virtue; the aspect of sin will gradually acquire stronger charms, and the grace of God, after a feeble resistance, will depart from his soul.

The argument taken from the respect due to this great mystery, which by some is held out as a motive to abstain from communion, though at first it may seem plausible, is, in fact, void of solidity and truth. The real and true glory of Jesus Christ in the blessed Eucharist, is best seen when He reigns over the hearts of His followers, and receives their adoration on the one hand, whilst He, on the other, sanctifies them with His adorable flesh, purifies them from vice, firmly establishes them in virtue, and at length transforms them into Himself. By frequent participation of this life-giving food we insensibly become celestial and divine, like our adorable Master; our thoughts are fixed on Him, and we no longer live but for Him. Whereas unfrequent communion directly tends to set bounds to the mighty power, which otherwise He would exert in our behalf in the Eucharist, and contracts that empire and dominion which He so justly claims over all the faculties of our soul. When we communicate but seldom, we gradually lose sight of His grandeur, and His infinite unchangeable beauty insensibly ceases to charm us. Our faith decays, our hope languishes, our charity cools, and Jesus Christ, in His sacrament, is presently neglected and forgotten; for though it be true, that there are other means of salvation besides frequent communion, it is not, however, less true, that frequent communion is of all others the most efficacious, and the best adapted to our weakness. This one source alone affords more abundant graces than all other means put conjointly together, and from this help alone we may become what we are created to be, good and perfect Christians; and as the possession of Jesus

Christ is what will constitute our eternal felicity hereafter in Heaven, so the present fruition of Him in His adorable sacrament, is the only thing which constitutes our happiness upon earth. Our common enemy, but too sensible of this important truth, is constantly at work to throw a veil over it, and strives, by every means, to obstruct a communication between frail man and this inexhaustible fund of every virtue and blessing.

The famous general of the Assyrian army, Holofernes, in the course of twenty days reduced the Bethulians to the greatest extremity of distress, by intercepting those channels of water which used to supply their wants, and by posting strong guards at every neighboring spring from whence they might draw relief. Not unlike to this stratagem is the artifice of the devil to withhold the unwary faithful from the water of eternal life, which incessantly flows from the blessed Eucharist; he surrounds, with strong guards, this living spring of the blood of Christ by obtruding a reverential fear that may make us dread an approach, and a religious awfulness that may make us stand at a distance; by this pernicious fallacy, thousands have fallen a prey to his tyranny, they have thirsted like earth without water, and have finally perished; thus has this adorable sacrament been as useless to thousands as if its institution had ever been a secret to them.

I dare further assert, that the supposed reverence or respect which withdraws from communion, has frequently even deviated into heresy against the real presence in the Eucharist, and from an opposition to this capital point of our holy religion, have some been led to oppose Christianity itself.

In fact, this false respect for communion, what does it naturally and generally lead to? At first it occasions an estrangement from the holy table, this estrangement brings on an indifference, indifference produces contempt, contempt, infidelity or unbelief in a point which is distinctly and authentically revealed.

During the ten first centuries of the Church, as communion was in frequent and even daily use, no doubt ever arose concerning the real presence of Jesus Christ in the Eucharist; the fathers and the faithful believed it with a liveliness of faith, which to this day excites our admiration; but when, unfortunately, communion began to be neglected, christian fervor also began to decline, and, in the eleventh century, Beringarius, Archdeacon of Angers, first, since the establishment of the Church of Christ, dared to call in question this capital article; he was not quite without adherents; his doctrine was, at three seperate times juridically and unanimously condemned, and he himself as often, but particularly on his death-bed, renounced and condemned it. Since the days of Beringarius this dogma of our faith (as a learned and judicious author observes) has been nowhere opposed, but where, through a depravation of morals, the belief and the use of the Eucharist had been on the decline.*

Experience sufficiently evinces that a *general* corruption of manners, is the necessary result of a general neglect of communion; the strong opposition which the Gospel meets with among men, the unbridled wantonness of youth, the inveteracy of vicious habits in advanced age, the general crimes which infest society, the loose, the libertine way of thinking, which in these days is held up as an ornament even to the name of a Christian, are to be ascribed to no other cause than to a neg-

---

* Quo ardentior erat fides in Ecclesia Catholica eo FREQUENTIOR erat usus hujus sacramenti. *Et inferius.* Licet animadvertere nunquam fuisse dubitatum de veritate corporis Christi, donec adeo refrixit ardor ille veterum Christianorum ut vix singulis annis communicarent. Maldonatus, lib. de sacr. Euch. conject. 10.

lect, followed by a disbelief of the advantages and necessity of frequent communion.

Is man then, at all times, to be a dupe to the wiles of the Serpent! At the creation, this malicious enemy brought ruin on our parents and their progeny, by prevailing on them to eat of the forbidden fruit; *eat, you shall not die, you shall be like gods.* They believed and transgressed the command of their Maker, they lost their innocence and their seat of bliss. And now, when Jesus Christ says to us, *eat of My flesh, and you shall have life everlasting.* The infernal fiend inverts the assertion, saying, eat not of the Eucharist, lest you should die. Alas! how many, from one motive or other, unfortunately listen to him! they eat not of this real fruit of life, and consequently they die.

CHAPTER II.

THE WORDS OF JESUS CHRIST WHEN HE INSTITUTED THE EUCHARIST, IMPLY FREQUENT COMMUNION.

LET the candid and impartial reader, figuring himself present at the last supper, attentively consider the significant words our blessed Redeemer made use of, in the institution of the adorable sacrament of the Eucharist; a few serious reflections on what was said on this solemn occasion, will, I doubt not, ascertain the doctrine of frequent communion. When Jesus Christ, by innumerable miracles, had proved His power and divinity in the face of His followers and of all Judea, on the eve of that memorable day which was to terminate His precious life, He proceeded on to the grand master-piece of all His wonders; and, having washed the feet of His twelve apostles, He took bread, lifted up His eyes to heaven, broke it, blessed it, and said, *take ye and eat, this is My body.** He also took the cup, and said, *drink ye all of this, this is My blood.*† Three of the evangelists relate this same event, in which,

---

* Matt. xxvi. 26.   † Ibid.

it is to be observed, Christ does not say, this is My body which you are to venerate and to adore, but *take ye and eat;* as if He would say, this is the great homage you are to pay Me; this is the use you are to make of My body, you are to make it your food, nay, your daily, or, at least, frequent food; for the general and obvious meaning of the word eating implies the taking of frequent nourishment. We commonly say of one who seldom takes nourishment, that he does not eat; and when a physician bids his patient to eat of such a food, there is no one who would not understand from thence, that that sort of aliment was to be his daily support. Besides, it is most creditable that our Redeemer gave us His adorable flesh as the frequent nourishment of our souls, from His having instituted this sacrament under the appearance of bread. For if our communions were intended to be unfrequent, why did He not, as He might have done, constitute His sacred body under the form of some precious remedy, or of some rare and delicate food? Remedies are seldom used, dainties are seldom eaten; while nothing is so common as to feed on bread, and, of course, nothing should be more usual to a Christian than to eat of the heavenly bread of the Eucharist.

This opinion receives light and confirmation from what we are taught to say in the Lord's Prayer, when we petition for our daily bread; our Savior terms this daily bread *supersubstantial*, or a bread above all substance,* which can be understood only of Jesus Christ himself, who is the celestial bread that came down from heaven; to imagine that we were here taught to confine our wishes to a material bread, and to sue for nothing more than what is needful to support this mass of clay and corruption, would be to form a supposition greatly unbecoming the belief of a Christian, and equally injurious to the wisdom of our Master. When we have prayed that the name of our heavenly Father may be adored and universally glorified by all, that we at last may be so happy, as to reign with Him in His everlasting kingdom, and that, to be made worthy of so exalted a favor, we may be submissive, whilst upon earth, to His blessed will, in the manner that the saints in heaven are actually conformed to it, we cannot doubt but the following petition regards that help and succor, which bears a proportion to so noble and dignified an end, and the bread we are bid to

---

* Matt. vi. 2.

ask for, is a bread *above all substance;* a bread,* which alone deserves the name of true food for man, because it is that bread alone that imparts heavenly life both to the soul and body of man; in short, it is Jesus Christ himself whom He would have us ask for, as the daily nourishment of our souls.

Let us proceed further, and still more amply trace the meaning of our divine Master. About twelve months before his passion, He solemnly promised to a great multitude of people, the institution of this great sacrament. *I am the bread of life,*† *the bread which cometh down from heaven. Your fathers did eat manna in the desert, and are dead. This is the bread which cometh down from heaven, that if any man eat of it, he may not die; and the bread that I will give, is My flesh for the life of the world, for My flesh is meat indeed.* The same doctrine does he inculcate in twelve different verses of the sixth chapter of St. John. From whence I reason thus; we take nourishment not only once in a year or even once in a week, but we feed ourselves *every day*, we

---
* **True bread** * * * **my flesh is meat indeed** * * * **He that eateth my flesh has everlasting life, and I will raise him up in the last day.**—[John vi.
† John vi. 48, 49, 52, 56.

eat bread daily; the Eucharist is truly our bread, it is meat indeed; what motive then can hinder us from concluding that it is designed and instituted for the *daily food* of our souls.

In the last mentioned chapter our divine Master minutely enlarges on every particular, He enforces His doctrine in the strongest terms, the words He expresses Himself in are as clear as they are energetic, and the whole of His discourse invariably insinuates frequent communion ; and that we may not doubt that such is His meaning, nor hesitate in our belief, that He even commands it, He at one time extols the excellency of this bread of life, of this bread that is come down from heaven, of this *bread,* he says, *which is My flesh;* at another time He promises rewards to those who shall eat of it, I will raise him; *he shall have eternal life;* and, again, lest the excellence of this bread, and the splendid rewards annexed to the eating of it should prove insufficient to bring us to an union with Himself, He proceeds to threats, by a most solemn assertion ;* and here we are to observe that it is a God who says, *My flesh is meat indeed;* and

---

* Amen, amen, I say unto you, except you eat of the flesh of the Son of Man, you shall not have life in you.

that the same God threatens, *unless you eat.* His offer must needs astonish us ; it is a prodigy of love; but His menaces are greatly alarming, for should we be less pliable to His request than it is His desire that we should, we infallibly must perish.

The comparison which He makes between this heavenly bread, and the manna which, for the space of forty years, fed the Israelites in the desert, cannot but attract the attention of every unprejudiced reader. The motive for the comparison seems obvious. The manna fell from heaven daily; it was gathered daily; and it was the daily food of that chosen people. The bread of life is Jesus Christ, who comes daily from heaven to feed his Christian people; it, therefore, is most expedient and proper that we should daily support ourselves with this heavenly nourishment. Can it be an easy matter to any mind, though never so captiously inclined, to misconstrue the meaning of our blessed Lord, into any other sense?

The above inference is still more solidly established when we reflect on the views our Redeemer proposed to Himself, by giving us this wonderful sacrament. His own glory, and our welfare and happiness, we believe, were what He had in view in this marvelous institution. He meant to furnish us with lasting and continued means of love and adoration, of praise and thanksgiving for the innumerable blessings which he continually bestows upon us, and this He particularly expresses immediately after the institution, *do this for a commemoration of Me,** as if He had said, that you may not too readily forget the many things I have done for you, and too easily lose the idea of My miracles, of My bounty and of My grandeur; to prevent this forgetfulness, to guard against your ingratitude, "I, invisibly indeed, but really will come and dwell amongst you; and as often as you receive me in the Eucharist, I will renew in your hearts the remembrance of all My wonderful works." Now, in supposition that we receive but seldom, there will be need of little argument to show, that we shall also seldom or never think either of Him or of His favors.

But the glory due our Redeemer is not alone the result from frequent communion; the happiness also of man, is equally connected with, and, in general depends on it. To be saved, we must be healed of our infirmities and weaknesses, we must be adorned with those virtues which our

---
* Luke xxii.

divine Master points out to us for practice; we must resemble Him, we must put on, nay, even transform ourselves into Jesus Christ, and become the living images of the Son of God. It is for these great purposes that He condescends to reside in the Eucharist, that by His habitual presence, he may continually cure us of our spiritual maladies, that He may afford us continual help and assistance, and that He may advance us daily to a nearer resemblance with the God of virtue and perfection. "Behold I am with you all days,* even to the consumation of the world."

Nor can it be said with any degree of propriety, or appearance of truth, that Jesus Christ would be equally honored, or that our welfare would be equally consulted, if, while he is exposed on our altars, and resides in our tabernacles, he should only be the object of our daily veneration; nothing indeed, is impossible to God, and therefore in His wisdom He might have annexed to an external worship, every means conductive to His glory, and beneficial to us. But it is not what His power can effect, that we are now in search of but precisely what our blessed Redeemer did mean and

---

* Matt. xxviii. 20.

intend when He instituted His sacrament, and what He daily means and intends by continuing to dwell amongst us. In His command, He lays no stress on our veneration, he mentions and insists only on a corporeal union: *Take ye and eat, this is My body; My flesh is meat indeed.* It is this manducation which he insinuates, and which he commands; to this, and to this alone does His promise extend, of diffusing in our hearts His sanctifying grace, and on this does He establish for Himself that supreme honor which He justly claims from His creatures. *If any man eat of this bread, he shall live forever.* And, *He abideth in Me and I in Him.** That is, he who eats My flesh shall have eternal life, by means of that grace which this divine food procures him; and this is man's greatest felicity; whilst we, by the same means, are allowed to reign in His heart, and this is our glory. Frequent, and even daily communion, is therefore the immediate and essential design of the institution of the Eucharist; for our Lord is ever desirous both to effect our salvation, and promote His own glory by giving us this daily food; for which reason He constantly

---

* John vi. 52, 57.

repeats what He said to Zacheus, *Make haste and come down, for this day I must abide in thy house.**

But what! will some one exclaim, is not the blessed Eucharist the greatest, the noblest of all sacraments; is it not there we approach the God of majesty and grandeur, whose judgments are terrible, whose justice is tremendous; a God before whom the angels themselves tremble, whilst they adore Him? And dare we believe that Jesus Christ would lavish Himself for our daily food; that He would have us feast daily at his adorable table? How incredible soever this truth may appear, we are not permitted to call it in question; and we shall facilitate our belief if we reflect, that though the old law was a law of terror and of justice, yet that which we have the happiness to live under, is a law of grace and of mercy. Our divine Legislator, upon every occasion, displays His boundless love for us, and all the merciful effects of His copious redemption. He would have the happy influence of His holy religion greatly to exceed the munificence and generosity of the famous Ahasuerus, whose pomp and magnificence were but a shadow and an imperfect type of what is effected in the Eucharist.

---
* Luke xix. 25.

We read in holy writ*, that this powerful monarch, to show forth his grandeur and riches, and to render conspicuous the glory of his reign, made a great feast, to which he invited all the grandees and nobles of his empire, the officers of his armies, and the most distinguished personages of every province throughout his dominions; the inhabitants also, from the highest to the lowest, of his vast and populous metropolis, were desired to partake of it. A royal magnificence shone forth on all sides, and on all sides were hung up sky-colored, green and violet hangings, guided by cords of silk and of purple, moving in ivory rings, and supported by pillars of marble. The beds also were of gold and silver, regularly placed upon floors paved with porphiry and white marble, which were beautifully embellished with paintings of wonderful variety. The meats were delicious, while most exquisite wines flowed in abundance from golden cups. Everyone had everything at will. This wonderful feast lasted a hundred and fourscore days; and the whole city of Shusan resounded with the praises of the bounteous and powerful Ahasuerus.

---

*Esther 1.

Jesus Christ speaking of His religion, and of the chief mystery it contains, which is the Eucharist, represents it to us, in two different places of the gospel, under the name of a great feast, to which many are invited. *A certain man made a great supper and invited many**.

This banquet of Jesus Christ, which ever way we consider it, is by far preferable to, and infinitely more magnificent than that of Ahasuerus: here, it is the King of kings, the sovereign Lord and Master of heaven and earth, who invited, not only the inhabitants of the town or country, but all nations and kingdoms of the world; and the meat which is put before them is nothing less than the adorable and precious body, blood, soul and divinity of Jesus Christ Himself. Instead of one place of resort there are numberless churches built, and sumptuous altars erected in all parts of the universe, where this feast is celebrated; and there is a still greater number of officers and ministers of this great King, whose sole employment is to dispose the faithful for this heavenly entertainment, and to distribute amongst them this bread of angels.

But what eminently distinguishes this feast above every other, and marks its peculiar charac-

---

*Matt. xxii. 2. Luke xiv. 16.

teristics, is the ever-flowing source of all graces and blessings. Here the faithful leisurely taste of every celestial delight, drink at the fountain of real felicity, and receive at each communion fresh pledges of eternal bliss. It is here also, where they praise and glorify the riches and munificence of the goodness of their God, where they incessantly admire the effulgence of his majesty and power, and gratefully acknowledge their distinguished happiness, in living under the dominion of so great and bounteous a king, while at the same time, they are fraught with a well-grounded hope of soon reigning with Christ in heaven. Thus would our Redeemer have His holy religion become a continual feast to every believer, for all such are His subjects, His friends, His brethren and His children. He seems to pay no regard to the consideration, that a frequent and constant communion with His creatures, might possibly lessen in them the respect which is due to Himself. On the contrary, His whole attention apparently inclines to obviate any slight on our part, of His most kind and all-bounteous invitation.

Ahasuerus would have justly taken offence if any of his numerous guests had shown an indifference to his royal condescension, he would have thought the dignity of his throne degraded into contempt, and his own personal merit sunk into dishonor. Any other conduct from his subjects, besides a grateful acceptance and a cheerful fruition of his favors, and that to the full extent of the meaning of their sovereign, as it inevitably would have reflected disgrace, inevitably also would it have excited resentment. A much greater injury is done to Jesus Christ the King of kings, as often as we, regardless of His invitation, and even disobedient to His express command, either totally absent ourselves from His royal table, or seldom approach near it. Our respect for so great a Master, as it admits of no kind of refusal, can only be manifested by a submissive obedience to His orders, and a ready campliance with His all-gracious will.

That such are His sentiments, He sufficiently declares from the parable in which He personates a certain man, who invited many to a great supper; the time for supper being at hand, he sent his servants to acquaint the guests that everything was in readiness; but they, from various motives, sent back their excuses; at which, the master of the house being angry, said to his servats, *Go out quickly into the streets and lanes of the city, and* *bring in hither the poor and the feeble, and the blind and the lame**. This being complied with, and there still remaining room, he sent a second time with this order, *Go out into the highways and behind the hedges, and compel them to come in that my house may be filled.* And finally, he pronounced this formidable sentence: *I say unto you, that none of those men who were invited shall taste of my supper†.* We read in St. Matthew a similar parable of a great king, who gave a great entertainment. From both which representations it is obvious to remark that, the former guests having slighted the invitation, both the king and the landlord sent for others at sundry times, and always with the greatest expedition and seemingly with a degree of impatience, which properly expresses the ardent zeal of Jesus Christ in favor of frequent communion, His zeal is roused even unto anger, and he considers their excuses as so many injuries offered to Himself. He moreover gives an order, to His servant, to *tell* the guests *that all is ready; go quickly and bring them hither,* adding, *compel them to come in,* and make use of a salutary violence, that my table may be full. This servant represents the ministers of

---
*Luke xiv. 21.   †Matt. xxii.

Jesus Christ, whose essential duty it is to persuade their flock to frequent communion, and when once they have engaged their wills into a compliance, they are next to dispose them for a worthy reception. From all which, we may most safely conclude, that Jesus Christ invites us most eagerly, commands us most peremptorily to communicate often, and threatens so rigorously in case of non-compliance, that the whole gospel relative to the Eucharist, seems but one continued sermon and precept to enforce frequent communion. From the considerations of the words of our Redeemer, let us proceed to His actions.

CHAPTER III.

THE ACTIONS OF JESUS CHRIST, WHICH RELATE TO THE EUCHARIST, IMPLY THE OBLIGATION OF FREQUENT COMMUNION.

THE works of our Redeemer are as instructive as His words, aud often express, after a more lively manner, His power, wisdom and bounty. "Our Lord," says St. Gregory, "instructs us sometimes by words, sometimes by actions, nay, His actions are often so many commands, because they tacitly point out to us the path which we are to follow*." In this chapter, two of our Savior's miracles shall come under inspection, which, from their different circumstances, will lay open to us His intention to establish frequent communion. The first of these is the multiplication of the five loaves, which preceded by twelve months the institution of the blessed Eucharist, and happened about Easter-time. The four Evangelists relate the fact in the following manner*: Jesus Christ, from

---

*Dominus Salvator aliquando sermonibus, aliquando vero operibus nos admonet, ipsa etenim facta ejus, præcepta sunt, quia dum tacitus facit aliquid, quid agere debeamus innotescit.--[Greg. Hom. 17. in Evan.

the summit of a mountain where He was seated, beholding a great multitude of people, took pity on them; He spoke to them concerning the kingdom of God, and cured the sick of their infirmities. As the day began to decline, His twelve apostles came and said to Him, "We are here in a desert place, and the time for refreshment is over, dismiss the people, that they may provide themselves with nourishment and lodging in the neighboring towns and villages; they have no occasion to move from hence, said our Lord, give you them to eat: and they said, we have no more than five loaves and two fishes, unless perhaps we should go and buy food for all this multitude. There were about five thousand men. And He said to His disciples, make them sit down by fifties in a company. They did so; and taking the five loaves and the two fishes, He looked up to heaven, and blessed them, and He broke, and distributed to His disciples to set before the multitude; and they all did eat, and were filled. And there were taken up of the fragments that remained twelve baskets. And those men, when they had seen what a miracle Jesus had done, said, this is of truth the prophet

---

*Matt. xiv. Mark vi. Luke ix. John vi.

that is to come into the world. Jesus, therefore, when He knew they would come to take Him by force and make Him king, fled again into the mountain alone by Himself."

This wonderful multiplication is unexceptionably one of the most conspicuous miracles we read of in the New Testament, and the singularity of it, as well as the importance of its tendency, is what most probably induced the four Evangelists to be so unanimeus and particular in the relation of it. It was not the manifestation of His goodness or power which our Savior had directly in view upon this occasion. At other times He had sufficiently convinced His followers of both the one and the other; His principal design here was to establish a fundamental doctrine of the religion He was come to preach, to facilitate the belief of it, and insinuate the daily advantages which were to accrue from it to Christian people. This capital point was the blessed Eucharist; and this miracle was a kind of preliminary and introduction to His subsequent discourse on the Eucharistical subject. It is in this sense that the holy fathers and interpreters understand and explain it*. And a little atten-

---

*S. Cyprianus Ep. 63. Aug. in Joan. 6. cit. a divo Thoma in Catena. Maldon. in Matt. xiv.

tion to the proceeding of our Redeemer, and to the method He takes to introduce His doctrine, will make it palpable and obvious.

The day after this prodigy, the multitude came in search of Him, and He, availing Himself of the astonishment they still were in said, * "You seek Me, not because you have seen miracles which prove My divinity, but because I fed you yesterday, and ye were filled. Labor not for the meat which perisheth, but for that which endureth unto life everlasting; and this food the Son of Man will give you. The people asked, What must we do to work the works of God? Jesus answered, You must believe that I am the Son of God. They again asked, by what miracle do you prove to us that you are the Son of God? Moses fed our fathers in the desert with a bread from Heaven, not only once as you have done, but for the space of forty years, work you a like miracle and we will believe in you." From these words of the Jews, the divine Jesus took occasion to raise their thoughts to the great mystery of the blessed Eucharist, in the following manner: "Moses did not give you a true bread from heaven, it was an aereal bread; My father gives you the true bread from

---
*John vi. 26.

heaven, for the bread of God is that which comes down from heaven and gives life to the world. His hearers, ravished with the excellency of this bread, cried out, Lord, give us *always* this bread." What expression could at once more plainly and more forcibly prove frequent communion, whether we consider the words of our Redeemer, or those of his hearers? These, on their side, demand a miraculous and daily nourishment, similar to that of the manna; and Jesus, on His side, acquiesces in their demand, and promises to give them this daily food, but a food by far more marvellous than the other, a food quite heavenly and divine. But how different soever this food may be from the manna, in respect to its excellence and the advantages it imparts, in the comparison they are on a level with regard to frequent and even daily communion.

It is further to be remarked, that our divine Lord never entered on any great mystery, without previously engaging the attention, and disposing the minds of his hearers by some wondrous works, which bore an analogy with his words, and with admirable wisdom he invariably adapted his actions, to the doctrine He was going to teach. Thus to confirm His ensuing resurrection, He frequently effected the resurrection of others, that His doctrine might receive force from the exertion of His power, and He Himself expresses it: "Now I have told you before it come to pass, that when it shall come to pass, you may believe*." And, if you will not believe me, believe my works†.

In like manner does He proceed in instituting the Eucharist. Through an excess of love for mankind, His desire is to feed them with His adorable flesh for their sanctification. The mystery is incomprehensibly great. Before He manifests His desire and all-bounteous intention, He astonishes His disciples and a multitude of people, by a striking miracle; this once performed, the wonder of feeding the universe with an eucharistical bread must occasion less surprise, from the evidence that thousands had actually been fed with a miraculous bread. The prodigy they were eye-witnesses to, must naturally incline the beholders to a belief of the other prodigy, which is promised to man for the life of the world. From these previous observations on the institution of the Eucharist in general, I now come to a particular disquisition into the intention of the frequent recep-

---

*John xiv. 29. †Ibid. x. 38.

tion of it. All, and each individual circumstance combine to assert it.

"Yesterday, said our Lord, you were fed with an earthly and corruptible bread; but I would have you look after a food that procures eternal life; this food the Son of Man alone can give you, and the Son of Man will give it you:" Here the comparison begins, let us trace it through every analogous circumstance which intervenes between the figurative miracle of five loaves, and that wonderful bread which was figured and typically represented.

Our divine Master looks down with compassion on a fatigued and famished multitude of people, and works a miracle to solace and refresh them; with an equal and ever attentive bounty and piteous concern had he long beheld the feeble and drooping universe on the brink of ruin, and through a superior and more lasting miracle, He proffers to the human race a heavenly nourishment, for their future support, which shall be efficacious enough at once to bestow life on them, and preserve it amongst them. His goodness leads Him to a sense of our wants, while His power enables Him continually to supply them.

He excites His disciples to relieve their fellow

creatures in distress: "You give them to eat;" in like manner does He actually inflame His ministers with the desire of administering His adorable sacrament. From the arrangement of the multitude into ranks of hundreds and fifties, we obviously discern the great care which is taken, that none should be deprived of the favor, or overlooked in the distribution. Similar is his attention to the universal distribution of the eucharistical bread, which He gives for the life of the world. The nations of the earth divided into dioceses and parishes, and headed by innumerable pastors, impartially share of this heavenly food, without distinction of rank or condition.

Bread, the most common human sustenence, is the matter of this miracle; and this same matter is used, consecrated, and exchanged into the body of Jesus Christ, to be the daily and common nourishment of our souls. The apostles are gifted with the power of multiplying the loaves in behalf of their brethren; the ministers of the altar consecrate daily; the eucharistic bread multiplies in their hands, the distribution of which is made with the greatest facility. The drift of the whole apparatus was the corporal refection of the people, and this refection is taken daily; the design of the sacramental bread, is the spiritual refection of our souls, of which we are daily in equal need. Our spiritual support therefore is the grand object which brought on the institution of this heavenly bread, which substantially contains the adorable flesh of our Redeemer. "The bread that I will give, is my flesh for the life of the world*."

This significant miracle, two months after, was followed and enforced by another, the nature and circumstances of which were, more or less, every way similar to those of the former. St. Matthew and St. Mark relate, that on this occasion, there were but four thousand men, inclusive of women and children, and that with seven loaves, which our Savior took, blessed, broke, gave to his apostles and they to the people, seven baskets were filled with the fragments, when they had been satiated.

The first of these two wonders, preceded our Saviour's promise of the Eucharist, as an introduction to so sublime a doctrine, and as an item of the exalted end for which it was designed. The second was subsequent to his bounteous promise, in order to corroborate and ascertain the truth and reality of it: both the one and the other were wrought within a twelve-month of that divine institution,

---

* John vi. 52.

and from the uniformity of their circumstances, they both clearly demonstrate, that Jesus Christ is that omnipotent God of nature, who has power to change bread into His adorable body, for the daily nourishment of those who love him, and that His mercy and goodness are equally conspicuous with His mighty power; while He renews* the remembrance of all His wonderful works, by giving a heavenly food to those who fear Him. He is desirous that this remembrance should be perpetuated to the latest times ; and observing that His apostles were growing unmindful of those two emblems of His unspeakable bounty, he reprehends their forgetfulness, and condemns their indifference. † "Do you not understand; neither do you remember the five loaves among five thousand men, and how many baskets you took up : nor the seven loaves among four thousand men, and how many baskets you took up ?"

Let us now examine our Saviour's apparition to the disciples of Emmaus, and the singular circumstances with which it was accompanied *. Our Lord, being seated with them at table, took bread, blessed it, and having broken it, gave it them to eat, when instantaneously they knew Him, while

---

*Psalm cx. †Matt. xvi. 9, 10.

He, as suddenly, vanished from their sight. They then said to each other, did not our hearts glow within us, whilst He was speaking to us on the road? They returned to Jerusalem, informed the apostles of the wonder, and that in the breaking of bread, their eyes had been opened. The same evening, whilst they were talking of these things, the doors being shut, Jesus stood in the midst of them, saying, "Peace be to you, it is I, fear not."

From all which it is obvious to observe, that Jesus Christ, when in company with His two disciples, consecrated the holy Eucharist. This seems to admit of no manner of doubt: for St. Luke, in the account he gives of this memorable fact, makes use of the same terms in which he, and the other evangelists express themselves, when they circumstantially relate the first institution of it. The authority also of tradition strongly supports the observation; to which St. Jerome adds, that in course of time the house of Cleophas was consecrated into a church, from its having been a place where our Lord had offered the eucharistic sacrifice, and distributed his adorable sacrament. It is also to be observed, that our blessed Redeemer, from amongst all His marvelous works, would

---
*Luke xxiv. 18.

choose to single out holy communion, as a proper means to manifest Himself to His followers, as a particular prodigy, which bore no resemblance with any of those miracles we read of among the patriarchs and prophets, and as a wonder which was the master-piece of all the wonders He had ever performed.

From these premises it is most natural to conclude, that our Saviour must have had communion greatly at heart, and that His zeal for asserting it must have been great and ardent, since on the day of His resurrection, He would consecrate and distribute the Eucharist, as if He would make known to the world that, at the time He asserted His divinity by virtue of His resurrection, He then also would ratify the reality of this sacrament, and confirm the use of it, which He had prescribed at the Cene. This further appears, from the testimony which the two disciples gave on their return to Jerusalem, when they alleged to the apostles, as the most incontestible proof of the truth of His resurrection, that they had known our Lord in the communion they received from Him; and while they were yet in conversation together on this subject, Jesus showed Himself to them, thus at once strengthening them in the belief both of His resurrection, and the reality of the Eucharist.

Whether then we consider the institution of the Eucharist, under the appearances of bread, which is a daily food ; whether we examine our Savior's express words, His parables or His miracles, either before or after His resurrection, we cannot reasonably doubt but it is the intention of Jesus Christ, that we should receive Him frequently in His sacrament, and that it is His delight to dwell among the children of men, whose greatest happiness it should be to live habitually in him, while He reciprocally lives in them.

CHAPTER IV.

THE DOCTRINE AND PRACTICE OF THE APOSTLES, AND OF THE PRIMITIVE CHRISTIANS, PROVE THE EXPEDIENCY OF FREQUENT COMMUNION.

IT will be readily granted, that the apostles were the best interpreters of the meaning and intentions of their Master, in every point of His doctrine, and consequently in that which concerns the Eucharist. They had frequently heard Him discourse on the subject, and all of them were present at the last supper. After the resurrection of our Lord, for the space of forty days, they received more ample instructions from Him, and being ascended into heaven, He sent them His holy spirit, who, in His unerring wisdom, taught them all truth, and enabled them to form the infant church perfectly on the plan, and in the spirit of their Master.

St. Peter, at the head of those founders of christianity, in two sermons, brought over to the faith eight thousand people, to these acceded a daily increase of believers, who, being initiated into the mysteries, by baptism, partook daily of the blessed Eucharist. This we find attested in the sacred history of the Acts of the Apostles, in two different places. *They were persevering in the doctrine of the apostles, and in the communication of the breaking of bread**. And further on, the sacred writer informs us, "That all the faithful were together daily in the Temple, breaking bread from house to house†, that is, receiving the blessed Eucharist, with simplicity and purity of heart, transported with joy, and thankful to God, and by this their charitable and meek behavior, becoming amiable to every beholder."

And here it is to be noticed, that the expression of breaking bread, is constantly employed by the inspired writers, to signify holy communion: it is an explanation given us by St. Paul, "The bread, which we break, *is it not* the partaking of the body of the Lord?"‡ even those who err in the belief of the real presence, in this point coincide with ecclesiastical tradition. It is also to be noticed, that the apostles went daily among the faithful to distribute the Eucharist, *daily breaking bread from house to house:* that this daily communion

---

*Acts, ii. 42. †Ibid ii. 46, 47. ‡I Cor. x. 16.

was the source of real joy and sincere gratitude, which broke forth into the praises of the Lord, and that it was preceded by great simplicity and purity of heart, while it was followed by a conduct charitable and irreprehensible.

This pre-supposed, I reason thus: the primitive Christians communicated daily, their teachers were the apostles: they persevered in the communion of every day, because they persevered in the doctrine of the apostles: therefore daily communion was an original document of the Christian religion, as it was delivered by the apostles to their followers. And this daily communion was the animation and soul of the primitive Church, the inexhaustible source from whence they derived their sanctity, and the life-giving food which formed them into heroes and saints. The authority of St. Paul adds weight to my argument, he was not at the institution of the Eucharist, nor was he one of the first twelve apostles. The Church was in being, and he, her persecutor, till the Lord appeared to him and wrought his conversion.

"This is what I hold from no man, but what I have immediately learned from the Lord, and what I also delivered faithfully to you. The Lord Jesus, the eve of His passion, took bread, broke it, gave thanks for the power which His Father had given Him over all things, and said, take ye and eat; this is My body which shall be delivered up for you : do this in remembrance of me*." In like manner He speaks of the chalice, and concludes by saying, "Do this as often as you drink my blood, for the commemoration of me."

Thus having related the institution of the Eucharist, in the same words that three of the evangelists make use of, the apostle reaffirms every part of the mystery, and with his usual energy annouces, that the eucharastic sacrifice shall represent the sacrifice of the cross, till Jesus Christ shall come to judge the living and the dead, and therefore shall continue to be offered daily, to the end of ages. †*As often as you shall eat this bread and drink the chalice, you shall show the death of the Lord, until He come.*

Here the apostle, like the other evangelists, faithfully repeats the sacred words of our Saviour, *Take and eat, this is My body.* Words which point out and determine the frequent reception of the Eucharist, as an habitual and daily nourishment. He also lays great stress on his Master's repeated

---

*1 Cor. xi. 23. †1 Cor. xi. 26.

command, of eating His body in remembrance of Him, which remembrance He specifies to be a lively representation of the death of our Lord on the cross, and is uninterruptedly to be continued to the last day of the world. It therefore follows, that communion also must be uninterrupted and daily, because in those days, it always was inseparable from the sacrifice, among the laity as well as the clergy.

The apostle, indeed, by assuring us that it is the body of our Lord, which we receive, would have us form the most exalted ideas of the blessing bestowed on us; he therefore warns us to be cautious and circumspect, lest, through unworthiness we should eat and drink, at this heavenly banquet, to our own ruin and condemnation: but He no where insinuates, that we are to abstain, or absent ourselves from it. In six different places, he enforces the duty of eating this bread, as an habitual and usual nourishment. The probation and self-examination, which He would have every one to enter upon, is prescribed only as a due preparation for frequent communion, and by no means intended as the least obstacle to the frequency of it. He therefore means that every Christian is first to take a survey of His interior, and when by a serious examination, he has prepared his soul, let him receive the body of our Lord : but if, in this scrutiny, he should discover that he is void of spiritual life, let him, by means of sacramental repentance, return to the state of grace, *and so let him eat of that bread:* in this, and no other sense is St. Paul to be understood, and in this sense is he universally understood by the Church, as we shall see hereafter.

Neither should we be deterred from frequent communion, because we are told, that we may receive unworthily, in not distinguishing this heavenly bread, from the bread which is common. The instruction which is here intended, is, that we are to receive this sacrament with a lively faith concerning the real presence of the humanity and divinity of Jesus Christ therein contained, and with a heart averse to, and disengaged from mortal sin. He who possesses this faith and purity of conscience, never can profane the body of Christ: nay, from the advice the apostle gives, of discerning the eucharistic from common bread, he points out that, when he wrote, communion was frequent and that he admonished the faithful, that although they communicated daily, they did not however receive common bread, but the adorable body and blood of Jesus Christ.

The practice of St. Paul, was consonant with his doctrine. His writings to the Corinthians, and many passages in the history of the infant Church, sufficiently prove it. In his first Epistle to the Corinthians, he deters the converted Gentiles not only from idolatry, but also from mixing with idolaters at their tables, where meats were served which had been offered to idols, and reasons thus: * "The chalice of benediction which we bless, is it not the communion of the blood of Christ? and the bread which we break, is it not the partaking of the body of the Lord? We all partake of the same bread; the things which the heathens sacrifice, they sacrifice to devils, and not to God, you cannot drink the chalice of the Lord, and the chalice of devils. You cannot be partakers of the table of the Lord, and the table of devils." From whence I infer: 1. That the Eucharist is the body of our Lord; *the bread which we break, is it not the partaking of the body of the Lord?* 2. That all eat the same bread; *we all partake of the same bread.* 3. That communion is an act of religious worship: *are not they, who eat of the sacrifice, partakers of the altar?* 4. That communion is a daily act of

---

* 1. Cor. x. 16.

this same worship: the apostle contrasts the eucharistical table, and the daily table of the idolaters, as if he said, you cannot sit down to the table of Jesus Christ in the morning, and to that of idolaters in the evening: *you cannot be partakers of the table of the Lord, and of the table of devils.* 5. I infer, that communion was in daily use; for he speaks of it, as of a daily action: *the bread which we break,* and in this he obeyed his Master: *take ye and eat.* Moreover, writing to the Hebrews, he says, * *We have an altar whereof they have no power to eat, who serve the Tabernacle.* There consequently was an altar for Christians; there was also a sacrifice; there was a partaking and a manducation of this sacrifice, and therefore there was a communion as frequent as the sacrifice, which was offered daily, as constant tradition clearly demonsrtates.

There are several other passages in the Acts of the Apostles, which strongly confirm the truth of my assertion. When the said apostle and Barnabas, were singled out by the Church of Antioch, for preachers to foreign nations, it was during the eucharistic sacrifice, which at that time was inse-

---

* Heb. xiii, 10.

parable from communion; that the Holy Ghost commanded the prophets and doctors of that church, to send Paul and Barnabas for the conversion of the Gentiles. * *As they were ministring to the Lord, and fasting, the Holy Ghost said to them, separate me Paul and Barnabas.*

We read also, that St. Paul never omitted any opportunity of celebrating mass, and of communicating the faithful. He was once at Troas, on a Sunday, where the Christians assembled to break bread, and to hear his instructions: as he was to depart the following day, he protracted his discourse till midnight †. The place of meeting was large, but well lighted up with lamps, and the congregation was numerous: among others there was a young man, by name Eutychus, who, probably, for want of room, had seated himself in a window, and being overcome by sleep, fell from the third story, and was taken up dead. Paul, moved to compassion, went to him directly, and brought him to life. He then returned to His functions, broke bread, consecrated, distributed the Eucharist, and departed early in the morning.

The fathers, especially St. Augustin, Baronius,

---

*Acts xiii, 2. †*Ibid*, xx. 7.

and the most respectable interpreters, are particular in observing, that the apostle of the Gentiles, even in his most hurrying and fatiguing journeys was most constant and assiduous in the consecration and distribution of the Eucharist; and that the Lord increased his zeal for frequent communion, by the above mentioned conspicuous miracle.

The apostle, St. Andrew, being urged to offer incense to idols, and renounce Jesus Christ, whose glory he was preaching, made answer to the proconsul Egeus, "I sacrifice daily on our altars to the only true omnipotent God, not the blood of oxen or of goats, but the immaculate Lamb; and when all the people have eaten of it, this Lamb remains whole and entire as at first *." We have this account from the priests and deacons of Achaia who were witnesses of his sufferings, and hearers of his speeches. Nor is it much to be wondered at, that he who had been so familiar with the sacrifice of the cross, should have been so passionately fond of dying on a cross, and that, being fastened to it, for the space of two days, he should have so eloquently preached the advantages and excellencies of it.

---

* In Martyrio a Presbyteris et Diaconis Achaiæ scripto.

CHAPTER V.

THE DOCTRINE AND PRACTICE OF THE ANCIENT FATHERS OF THE CHURCH, PROVE ALSO THE EXPEDIENCY OF FREQUENT COMMUNION.

THE primitive Church was formed by the apostles only. Nor was she ever more worthy of our respect and imitation than in those happy days of innocence and purity of heart, of union with God, of real and true zeal for His honor and glory. Nay, we can only be deemed followers of Jesus Christ, from our resemblance to those fervent souls. The spirit of Jesus Christ, died not with the apostles; the Church has carefully preserved it, and transfused it down to our times, and with equal steadiness and zeal will continue to the end of the world, to teach the necessity and advantage of frequent communion. We shall see, in the sequel of this treatise, that the ancient fathers, the doctors of the Church, the councils, the popes, and the saints, unanimously agree in this particular.

The canons which are ascribed to the apostles, are, without doubt, of great antiquity, and, with reason, are supposed to comprise the prevailing Church discipline of those days. We read in the ninth canon, the following regulation. * "If a clerk, after having made the oblation, should not communicate, he must show cause for his omission, that he may stand clear in the eyes of the public; but should he refuse to apologize, or should his apology be insufficient, let him be excommunicated for the scandal he has given." And the tenth canon imports, "That those among the faithful, who go to church without communicating, are to be excommunicated for breeding disturbance in the house of God." From whence it is obvious to conclude, that in those early times, it was singular and extraordinary for any of the faithful to be present at the holy mysteries, without partaking of them, and that a nonparticipation was construed into a scandalous disturbance.

St. Ignatius Martyr, the third bishop of Antioch, in succession to St. Peter, says in his fourteenth letter, "Be zealous, and approach frequently to the holy communion, that glorious mystery of divine power and love †.

---

*Quos citant Cabass et innummeri authores. † Festinate ergo frequenter accedere ad Eucharistiam et gloriam Dei. S. Ign. Ep. 14. sub finem.

The philosopher and martyr St. Justinus, who lived in the middle of the second century, writes as follows, in his second apology to the emperor Antoninus, * "On every Sunday or Lord's day, the Christians, both in the towns and country villages, assemble in one place of worship: the Eucharist is given to every one present, and is sent by deacons to those who are absent." We cannot well form a more lively idea than is here given us; of the zeal which animated the primitive pastors for the frequent distribution of the Eucharist, as it was universally extended to all those, whether present or absent, who professed the law of Christ. They assembled indeed but once a week, which was owing to the persecutions they generally were under: however, on the days of meeting, besides universal communion, there was a distribution made of the same heavenly bread, among the congregated members, which they carefully took home with them, and which during the week, when fasting, they received in private. Tertullian, among others, informs us of this, where he says, "†The daily bread which we ask for, is the body of Jesus Christ, which we wish to be al-

---

* Distributio et communicatio quæ fit eorum in vuibus gratiae actæ sunt praesenti, absentibus per Diaconos Mittitur. Justin. Apol. 2. prope finem. † Tertul. de Orat. Dom. c. 6.

ways with us, and from which we are always unwilling to be separated." And elsewhere, the same Tertullian, dissuading his wife from marrying a heathen, should she become a widow, writes, " *The more pains you will take to conceal yourself, the more suspicious will you become to heathenish curiosity : will you conceal the sign of the cross, which you make on your bed and on yourself? and when you will have to rise in the night time for prayer, will not your husband discover what you secretly eat, previous to any other food? and, should he find it to be bread, would he not suppose it to be that bread which is spoken of?" Here communion in former times, is represented to us as a custom, not less frequent, than rising in the night to prayer. It was consecrated bread which the above mentioned woman received every morning, before she took any other nourishment, and therefore it evidently follows, that in the primitive ages, private and daily communion was allowed of, encouraged, and universally practiced.

To the testimony of Tertullian, I join that of Origen; they were contemporaries in the third

---

* Idem L. 1. ad Uxorem c. 5.

century. * "If we do not eat the bread of life, if we do not nourish ourselves with the flesh of Jesus Christ, if we drink not His blood, if we slight our Redeemer's heavenly banquet, we ought to reflect that, though God is all-bounteous, He is equally just, and will punish us for our neglect." Here the words eating and nourishing, seem sufficiently to indicate the frequent and constant use of the blessed Eucharist.

Eusebius, of Cesarea, is still more explicit: † "The priests indeed, by "their renewing *every day* the memory of the body, and blood of Jesus Christ, are devoted to a sacrifice, and to a ministry, which is by far more excellent than that of the Old Testament."

St. Cyprian, who also lived in the same century with the above mentioned fathers. ‡ "We pray that this bread may be given us *daily*, lest we, who actually live in Jesus Christ, from a *daily* use of the Eucharist as a food of salvation, should unfortunately, through the perpetration of any grievous offence, become unworthy of this heavenly

---

* Orig. hom. 88, in Luc.   † Euseb. demonst. Evang. L. 2. c. 10.
‡ Hunc panem dari nobis *Quotidie* postulamus. ne qui Eucharistiam *Quotidie* ad cibum salutis accipimus, intercedente graviori delicto, dum abstinentes et non communicantes a celesti pane, prohibimur, a Christi corpore separemur. S. Cypr. Serm. de Orat. Dominica.

bread, and by this means be separated, as unworthy members, from the mystical body of Christ."

The Eastern perfectly agrees with the African and primitive Church. St. Chrysostom tells us, * "He who is free from mortal sin, may communicate *daily*. The only grief of a Christian is, to be deprived of this heavenly nourishment." And elsewhere, "I mean to say all in one word, which word is extremely important as well as salutary. Neither is it I, but the holy spirit, who shall speak to you: several among you partake of the holy mysteries but once a year; some twice, others oftener: this concerns you all, as well as those who are present, as those who live in deserts: I neither approve of those who receive only once, nor of those who communicate oftener: but only of those who communicate with purity of conscience, let all such communicate constantly." †

The same on the Epistle to Timothy. How, do you say, can these evils come upon us, for we receive this sacrament but once in a twelve-month? But it is from this very source that your misfortune takes its rise: you estimate your merit, not from

---

* Chrys. hom. 8. in Matth. † Qui cum mundo corde, *semper* accedant. Chrys. hom. 17. Ep. ad. Hebr. circa medium.

purity of soul, but from the distance of time between your communions : and you fancy, that you can shew no greater respect, nor pay greater homage to the sacrament, than by your unfrequent appearance at this heavenly table. There is no doubt, but one unworthy communion, exposes us to eternal punishment, whilst, on the contrary, we secure our salvation by a worthy reception, though our communions be most frequent. What motive then should induce us to measure our communions by the laws of time? it is purity of heart that should chiefly determine them : this mystery is not greater or more respectable at Easter, than at any other season: it is at all times the same, at all times the same victim." This was the reasoning of the great Chrysostom ; from whence I conclude, that he who is free from sin, may communicate daily : that the privation of this sacrament, should be the sole cause of grief in a Christtian; that recluses, and others, who, through respect, think it proper to abstain from it, are mistaken, and deluded: that purity of conscience should regulate our conduct in this particular: and finally, that unfrequent communion disturbs the Church, and produces every disorder.

St. Ambrose confirms this universal doctrine

concerning communion.* "If the Eucharist be a daily bread, why do you receive it but once a year? Receive it *daily*, that it may profit you *daily*."

St. Jerom, that great luminary of the Eastern and Western churches, a man of genius, no less sublime than enlightened, in his letter to Licinius, writes as follows: "You ask whether you should communicate *every day*, it being asserted, that such is the practice of the churches of Rome and of Spain: if your conscience be pure, receive the Eucharist daily, nor yet censure us: listen to the saying of the psalmist, *taste, and see how sweet the Lord is*." † From the above quotation it is clear, that in the Roman and Spanish churches, daily communion was customary, and that the saint's advice to his friend was in favor of this custom, without condemning the practice, which, in those days prevailed in the East, of communicating but thrice a week, viz: on Fridays, Saturdays and Sundays.

The same doctor elsewhere informs us, that the Christians in Rome, both married and single, communicated *every day*, not only during their public assemblies, but frequently also in private, and at their respective homes ‡.

---
* Si quotidianus panis, cur sumis post annum? accipe *Quotidie*, quod tibi, prosit *Quotidie*. 1. 5. c. 4. de sacram. † Epist. ad Licinium.
‡ T. 1. Apol. c. 6. in Jov. ad Pammachium Ep. 52.

St. Hilarius, whose life and writings adorn the Gallican church, accedes to the authority of the rest of the fathers. "Give us," he says, "our *daily* bread; God desires nothing more, than that Jesus Christ should live daily in us: for He is the bread of life, the bread that is come down from heaven. And as this demand is a *daily* one, we therefore petition, that it may be given us *daily*." The above words we find quoted in the Council of Toledo, from whence it is evident that both the Spanish and Gallican churches were unanimous on the article of daily communion.

St. Augustin in his fifty-fourth letter to Januarius says, "Some receive *every day* the body and blood of our Lord; some receive him on certain days in the week: there are places in which no day passes without offering; and there are others, where they only offer on Saturdays and Sundays: from whence it is proper to conclude that these sort of customs allow of a discretionary liberty, and that a prudent, discreet Christian can follow no better rule than that which prevails in the church where he is.

The sole point in question here relates only to different customs of different places, either of daily communion, or of communion but on some days in the week, both which he approves of, and determines the prevailing practice of every place, to be the best rule for the conduct of its respective inhabitants. But he all along supposes, that where communion does not prevail daily, it prevails at least oftener than once a week. He then continues to say: "However, where the sins committed are not so great, as to deserve excommunication, no one should deprive himself of the *daily* remedy of the body of our Lord." The same saint is still more explicit in his sermon to the newly christened. * "It is your duty to know what you have received, what you do receive, and what you are to receive *daily*: the bread you see on the altar, being sanctified by the word of God, is the body of Jesus Christ."

S. Bernard, one of the greatest ornaments of the age he lived in, and the last on whom the title of father of the church was conferred, thus writes: † "He, who is wounded, seeks a remedy; we are wounded by sin, sin is a wound, for which the sacrament of the Eucharist is the best remedy; receive it therefore *daily*, and you will meet with a

---

* Serm. 227. ad Infantes.   † Bern. Serm. in Cen. Dom.

daily cure." And lower down in the same sermon on the Lord's Supper, we read: "The friends of the spouse, many worthy prelates and abbots, many pious and virtuous souls have relished, nay, and have made a thorough experiment of what I advance, and for this reason they *most frequently* feed at the holy table."

Antiquity, therefore, universally asserts and teaches both frequent and daily communion: the true oracles of religion clearly decide the question: the most enlightened of the East and West unanimously proclaim to the world that the Eucharist is the real and daily bread of Christians.

And this doctrine was not only preached, but was also universally practiced during the first twelve centuries. As to the first five we can entertain no doubt about it. S. Justin, S. Cyprian and Tertullian bear witness in favor of the second and third centuries. S. Jerom, S. Chrysostom and S. Augustin, are vouchers for the fourth and fifth: and the rest of the fathers, including S. Bernard, sufficiently prove that the same practice prevailed in after ages. In former times, communion was given immediately after baptism. And we learn from S. Cyprian,[*] that even sucking children par-

---
[*] Cypr. de Lapsis. Tertul de Corona, c. iii.

took of this sacrament: and both he and Tertullian inform us that it was usual to offer up the sacrfice of the mass twice a day, morning and night.

In times of persecution, when frequent meetings became dangerous, the faithful took home in baskets consecrated bread, and privately partook of this precious treasure. In consequence of this practice, we read in S. Cyprian, of a woman, who, being in the state of sin, went to open a box or basket which contained the sacred body of our Lord, from whence a sudden flash of fire darting forth, greatly alarmed and terrified her.

Nicephorus, Gregory of Tours, and Evagrius,[*] inform us that it was a prevailing custom in the church, frequently to give communion to people of all ages, not excepting children. And when the assembly was over, which was held on certain days in the week for general communion, it was the practice of the Greek Church, especially that of Constantinople, to call in from school those children who were fasting, among whom were distributed the consecrated fragments. Nicephorus tells us, that he himself had often been of the

---

[*] Niceph, l. 17. c. xxv. Hist. Eccles. Greg. de Gloria Martyrum c. viii. Evagr. Hist. Eccles. l. 4. c. xxxv.

tells us that he himself had often been of the number, and adds the following memorable event.

A Jewish child, joining some of his companions who were going to communion, communicated also. His father, a glass-maker by trade, understanding what had passed, threw his child into a burning furnace. The mother, ignorant of her husband's cruelty, was inconsolable at the loss of her son. For the space of three days she was restless in the search of him, and wherever she went, joined to her sighs and sobs loud repetitions of his name. While in this distracted condition, she chanced, on the third day, to be near the furnace, from whence the boy answered to her call: she heard, she flew, she opened it, and to her great astonishment found him as safe and well as if he had been placed on a bed of roses : he said, that a lady of surprising beauty, had all along taken care of him, had given him necessary nourishment, and that by throwing water repeatedly on the fire, she at last had extinguished it. The emperor Justinian, at the earnest request of both mother and son, gave orders for their baptism : while he sentenced to death the hard-hearted father, who persisted, to the last, in his obstinacy.

In the records of antiquity, we everywhere discover a peculiar attention in bishops in general, to promote among the faithful, fervor and devotion to holy communion: and everywhere do they express even an anxious desire to have it decently preserved, and, as occasion offered, duly distributed. The first general council, held in the fourth century,* earnestly recommends the keeping of the Eucharist in public churches, that the wants of the faithful, whether sick or in health, may be readily supplied.

In the council of Tours we read,† that the body of our Lord is by no means to be ranked with church images, but reverently to be placed under the cross: and that during the month of August, mass was to be celebrated early in the morning; because in that month there were many holidays, on which all the faithful assisted at the holy sacrifice, which was appointed to be offered early in the day, that the harvest might not be neglected.

Now it is well known, that in those days, mass was very seldom said anywhere, without communion on the part of every assistant.

The council of Auxerre ‡ determines, that when women receive the body of our Lord, they must

---

* Nicen. 1. c. 13. † An. 566. ‡ An. 636.

have on their Sunday's head-dress, or a linen veil; and that they are to put off receiving till the following Sunday, should they, through any accident, come unprovided with it.

St. Isidore, a Spanish bishop, who died in the seventh century,* compiled minutely the ceremonies of the Mozorabic mass for every day, and determined the method of saying it during the different seasons of the year; among many remarkable things contained in this work, we find that when the priest, reciting the Lord's prayer, had pronounced these words, *give us this day our daily bread*, the clerk made answer, *which is no other than thyself, O Jesus Christ*. From whence it is obvious, that in the seventh century, the Eucharist was looked upon as the daily bread of the faithful.

Near the end of the same century, St. Theodore, archbishop of Canterbury, died in England. He was the first among the Latins who composed a penitential book, in which he observes, that the laity among the Greeks communicated every Sunday, and that those who absented themselves from the

---

* Ibid.

holy table three Sundays following, received sentence of excommunication.

During the eighth century, Theodulphus, bishop of Orleans,* in his instructions to his priests, chapter the fourth, expresses himself thus: "All, who are not under excommunication, are to receive the sacrament of the body and blood of Jesus Christ every Sunday in Lent, on Thursday, Friday, and Saturday in holy week, and also on Easter Sunday. The whole week of Easter is to be solemnized as on Easter-Day. For as it is dangerous to approach this sacrament unworthily, so also is it dangerous to abstain from it for any time; excepting those who, being excommunicated, do not communicate at pleasure, but only at certain times; excepting also many pious persons, who communicate almost *daily*."

We read in the fourth council of Tours, which was held in the ninth century*, that "The laity were under strict precept of communicating three times a year. And the priests were forbidden to distribute at the end of mass, the body of our Lord indiscriminuately to children, and to every one who presented himself, lest some should re-

---

* An. 786.   † An. 813.

ceive in the state of sin." From whence we cannot but conclude, that the then prevailing custom among the faithful was, to communicate when the mass was over, at which they had assisted.

The tenth and eleventh centuries abounded with churches throughout the Christian world, and their respective priests increased in proportion. Many abbeys were founded, in Hungary, by St. Stephen, king, in France by king Robert, and in Germany by St. Henry, emperor; the abbey of Cluny was instituted by Bernon, who was its first abbot; and the bishops St. Dunstan, in England; St. Boniface, in Germany; St. Adelbert, in Bohemia, universally set the example of frequent communion, and zealously enforced it in the respective monasteries, dioceses, kingdoms, and empires in which they lived.

From the above proofs I mean to infer, that the doctrine of frequent, and even daily communion, is a most constant, clear, and general tradition of all churches; that it has been invariably and universally practiced by all good Christians; that this practice was formerly more prevalent, than it is in our days; that the apostles, bishops, priests and deacons, carried the Eucharist about with them to Christian dwelling-houses, and to prisons; that the faithful kept it at their respective homes, and took with them in their travels, this sacred depositum; and therefore, that the assertion is false, which denies that frequent communion was not universally taught, encouraged, and practiced during the ten first centuries of the Church of Christ.

CHAPTER VI.

THE DOCTRINE AND PRACTICE OF THE LEADING SCHOLASTIC DOCTORS, CONCERNING THIS SUBJECT.

From the authority of the fathers of the Church, I proceed to that of her scholastic doctors, who, for their profound learning and pious erudition, deservedly attracted the attention, and excited the admiration of the ages they lived in, and still continue forcibly to claim the respect and veneration of succeeding generations. It cannot but be productive of a heart-felt joy in the breast of every true follower of Christ, to behold this most respectable body of men, made up of the most improved, refined, and brightest geniuses, unison in their language, unanimous in their sentiments, and invincible in their arguments in support of the propriety, excellency, and advantage of frequent communion.

I begin with St. Thomas, who moves the following question: "*Is it lawful to communicate

---
* S. Tho. Sum.

every day? I answer, "that, on account of the virtue and efficacy of this sacrament, it is advantageous to receive *daily.*" He then quotes St. Ambrose, as quoted in the preceding chapter, when speaking of one who receives this sacrament, he says, "If he be prepared to receive every day, it is extremely laudable that he should." He then proceeds to the solution of the following objections: Baptism is administered but once: the Paschal Lamb was eaten but once in a year: the Centurion pleased our Lord, when, through respect, he entreated him to forbear coming under his roof. "Baptism he owns, which is the sacrament of our spiritual regeneration, is not reiterated, because we are born but once: whereas the Eucharist, which is the spiritual nourishment of our souls, is taken daily, as we do the material nourishment of of our bodies." To the second objection he replies, "The Paschal Lamb, figure of the passion of Jesus Christ, and of this sacrament, was eaten but once a year; but the Eucharist is a memorial of the passion by way of nourishment and nourishment must be frequent." To the third objection, he answers, "The Centurion, through respect, was unwilling that Jesus Christ should enter under his roof; Zaccheus, on the contrary, received him with joy: they both honored our Lord, the one by his respect, the other by his love: but love, joined to confidence, is preferable to timidity and fear; almost everywhere in scripture, we are exhorted to confidence and love."

Next to St. Thomas, I place the seraphic Doctor Bonaventure, who writes, "*It must be said, that if you be in the state of the primitive Church, (that is in the state of grace) your daily communion is praiseworthy and commendable." And elsewhere; "†He who is always prepared, always receives this sacrament to advantage: wherefore the primitive Christians received every day because they were holy." The holiness which is here alluded to, is no other than the actual state of grace. We read in the works of the same saint, "‡It is beneficial and salutary to a Christian soul to prepare herself for the frequent use of this remedy: and though there should be a degree of coldness or tepidity, she, confident in God's mercy, should not refrain from it: for you unite not yourself to Jesus Christ, that you may sanctify him, but that he may sanctify you: communion therefore is not to be omitted, though we should be deprived of all sensible devotion." I place this

---

* S. Bon. T. I. de exam. Doctr. † Id. in 4. Distinct. 12. ‡ De prof. Relig. l. 2. c. penult.

saint at the head of the whole order of St. Francis, and of the innumerable list of doctors and other teachers, who have distinguished, and continue to distinguish themselves for their zeal in asserting frequent communion.

Father Cyprien of the Nativity, of the order of Carmelites, has translated a Spanish book, the drift of which is, to ascertain daily communion. He in particular observes, that it is the right of children to sit daily at their father's table: in support of this right, he urges the authority of the fathers, the arguments of the scholastics, and the example of the saints, and proves that nothing but a mortal blemish on the soul, can deprive her of her privilege.

Denis, the Carthusian, and Molina, a Carthusian also of Spain, have written on the same subject, and both decide in favor of frequent, and even daily communion: the testimony of these two alone, sufficiently determines the sense of that holy order at large, which, to this day, universally keep up the practice of daily communion.

The order of our Lady of Mercy, is not inferior to any other in doctors, who have published valuable and perfect treatises on frequent communion. Witness the celebrated Villa-Roel, a Spaniard, and the great Falconi, author of the book entitled, *Our Daily Bread.* This production is a masterpiece for the force and energy of his arguments, which strongly prove the Eucharist to be truly and properly the daily bread of Christians, nor is the sweetness and delicacy of his style, which particularly characterizes the author, inferior in any degree to the strength of his reasoning.

I cannot omit Father Giry Provincial in the order of Minims, who, in a discourse on the feast of the blessed Eucharist, displays the greatest zeal and erudition in favor of frequent communion. He alleges the custom of the primitive Christians, the opinion of the ancient fathers, of the doctors and saints, and particularly of the learned Taulerus, and the pious Blosious, the latter he quotes in the following manner: " * A great and sensible devotion, is by no means requisite for frequent communion. Let no one therefore, under pretense of any small fault or failure, withdraw himself from the benefit of the holy Eucharist; but, on the contrary, let him who is weak and imperfect, be of good heart, and go to this holy table with joy and with love."

---

* Blof. l. de Sacram. c. 6.

Suarez, a divine, no less holy than learned, treats this subject with equal piety and precision: "* It is not forbidden by any law either human or divine, to communicate EVERY DAY. Daily communion was practised in primitive times, and at all times *frequent* communion, being consonant with the unanimous sentiment of divines, ought to be recommended and encouraged." He then, in support of his assertion, brings in the testimony of the fathers; and adds, "A worthy communion is, in itself, a commendable action, but it cannot be commendable to refrain from it: a frequent reception of this sacrament, originates from charity as from its basis and principle, whilst fear or negligence must actuate those who abstain from it: and as there is no doubt but the work of charity greatly excels the influence of fear, it is equally true, that a FREQUENT communicant greatly surpasses another, who is not so assiduous: the repeated fruits and advantages which accrue to him from the sacrament, decide the superiority, exclusive of other personal merits which may level him with, or raise him above the fearful or indolent Christian."

---

* T. 3. Disp. 79. Sect. 3. Disp. 63. sect. 3.

Cardinal Toletus, in the instruction he gives to priests, and in the nineteenth chapter of his sixth book on frequent communion, forcibly proves it to be equally laudable and beneficial. "As it is the food of the soul, the use of it of course, should be common and habitual. We also constantly stand in need of it: for it is instituted for the remission of venial sins, the commission of which slackens and diminishes charity; it is also intended as a preservative against mortal sin: man frequently falls into the former, and is DAILY exposed to the danger of the latter: the remedy therefore to the one, and the defense against the other should be in constant use. We know from experience, that many, from a vicious and dissolute course, have, by means of FREQUENT communion, so reformed their conduct and manners, as either to sin no more, or very little, the remainder of their lives."

I say nothing of the great Petavius, who, to this day, attracts an eye of admiration, even from the most learned, and who has particularly distinguished himself by his conclusive refutation of the Arnould, who stood up against frequent communion; and shall pass to Algerius, a Benedictine monk of the order of Cluny, one of the most celebrated men of his age, and a most zealous defender of the Eucharist in the twelfth century. The opinion of this learned writer, relative to our present subject, will sufficiently establish the general sentiment and doctrine of his respectable order.

"* Although the oblation of Jesus Christ on the cross was made only once for the salvation and redemption of all, nevertheless, this same oblation is DAILY necessary, in order to comfort man and strengthen him in his frailty, whereby he falls daily, and is tempted to sin mortally, or venially at least....and we, with the help of this victim, obtain, not only the remission of our sins, but also shelter and protection from every temptation. For when the enemy of our happiness observes, that, from a participation of this incomparable mystery, the avenue of our heart is taken up with the splendor and majesty of the king of heaven, and that Jesus Christ has his abode within us, he speedily withdraws, and is readily put to flight."

The same Author in the twenty-second chapter of the same book, adds: "But if it be dangerous to receive, or not to receive this heavenly medicine, what is to become of us? Let no human infirmity despair, though encompassed with so many diffi-

---

* Alger. l. I. de Sacram. Euch. c. 16.

culties: S. Agustin opportunely comes to our assistance: he leaves to every one's option, either to receive EVERY DAY, or only several times in the week; although to abstain a long while from the Eucharist, is, doubtless, a great detriment to salvation, whether our motive proceeds from an obstinate attachment to our own opinion, or from carelessness and neglect of this sacrament. St. Hilarius, compassionating on this occasion, the weakness of the imperfect and of beginners, gives them the following counsel, let no one be diffident of God's grace; but he who has left off sinning, let him not leave off communicating."

To the above authorities, I join those of several learned and holy French divines, such as Gerson, Baily Isambert, Duval and Gamache. Gerson, who was chancellor of the university of Paris, and much famed for his numerous works of piety, in his Preparation for Mass, says, "The sacraments are remedies, the sick and infirm approach to Jesus Christ, and provided that you are free from mortal sin, go to him VERY OFTEN: the man who comes to this table cold and wanting in devotion, returns from it refreshed and fervent." And in his ninth Treatise on the *Magnificat*, he says, "Considering the effects of this sacrament, it is much more commendable to receive it often through love, and with confidence in the mercies of God, than to excommunicate one's self from it in some measure, through fear and scruple;" and further on, "The fear and respect which withholds us from the Lord who calls and invites us to come to him, is unreasonable and even foolish."

Bail also, a doctor of Paris, and subpenitentiary of the cathedral, expresses himself as follows: * "If directors of souls are not very prudent, they may here easily fall into a mistake, by rashly withholding their penitents from FREQUENT communion, the fruits of which are by far greater and more numerous than it is possible to express or even to conceive." And elsewhere he adds: "Too great an interval between one communion and the other is extremely dangerous, because, most commonly, it is fruitless; that respect, which so long separates us from God, is neither right nor commendable: it should not withdraw us from, but excite us to go, and be united to him. If then directors are not on their guard, they may err much, and grievously offend God, by keeping souls back from the sacrifice of the Lord."

---

* De Tripel. Examp. p. 3, q. 8.

He then quotes several of the holy fathers, who condemn a long absence from communion, and S. Augustin in particular, who would have it left to every one's option of communicating daily: and concludes with the opinion of Mathias Hauzeur: "All Christians who are not rendered unworthy by mortal sin, have received a right from Jesus Christ and his church of communicating DAILY: this right is derived to them from the sacrifice at which they are present. To dissuade one from communion, on account of a bad conscience, is a very different thing from that usurped authority which most indiscreetly and tyrannically deprives the faithful of this their divine right." It seems, however, to be a prevailing sentiment among divines in general, that when time and circumstances will admit of a delay, a great sinner though absolved from his sins, should for a while be deprived of communion, but this restriction should in prudence be confined to a short space of very few days. Isambert and Duval agree in sentiment and expression with the above doctors, quotations therefore from them may be deemed superfluous: but I cannot conclude this chapter without strengthening the argument of it by the weighty suffrages of two very celebrated names, S. Anselm, archbishop of Canterbury, and the great Fenelon, archbishop of Cambray: the former was a bright ornament to the justly renowned order of Benedictine monks, and one of the most learned primates England ever saw. From his excellent treatise on the Sacrament of the Altar, I shall select only a few words, which however, contain in substance the scope and conclusion of the whole work. " * He who loves God most, eats oftenest of his food, and reciprocally, the oftener he eats this food, the greater is his love." The latter named prelate was a man whose sublime genius and deep penetration, whose singular talents, erudition and piety, will ensure him the love and admiration of the latest posterity. The beauty and solidity of his writings, but particularly his most amiable virtues, which, with equal energy and tenderness of devotion beam from every line, will ever exhibit him to view in the fairest and brightest colors; and if, in his treatise on the maxims of the saints, a single shade of human fallibility intervened, which, for a moment, rendered so great a character less conspicuous, the apparent blemish, originated from an excess of charity and inattention, was presently removed by

---

* Hunc cibum plus manducat, qui plus amat: & rurfus qui & plus manducat, plus et amat, l. 5. de Sacram. Altaris.

his exemplary submission, which added more lustre to every shining virtue he possessed, than if he had never given proof, in one instance of his life, that he, like every other individual, was liable to mistakes. This illustrious author, in his book on Frequent Communion, writes in the following manner: "The case in question is, of a Christian whose conscience is pure, whose conduct is regular, and who sincerely and candidly submits himself to a discreet and prudeut director: this Christian, in himself languid and weak, avails himself, for support and vigor, of the celestial manna: he is imperfect, but his imperfections displease him, and therefore he takes pains to remove them. I say, that a good and truly wise director may and ought to induce him to almost DAILY communion: for we are taught by the fathers, that the Eucharist is our DAILY bread; that Jesus Christ gives himself to man under the appearance of bread, a food, which with man is the most in use, that man may become accustomed to his resuscitated and glorious body. The institution also of this sacrament, as tradition explains it to us, strongly invites us to it. The Christians of early times, and even such as were immediately under the care and inspection of the apostles, were not free from imperfections, yet all were unanimous in frequently breaking bread: the good therefore and virtuous of our days, may, after their example, be constant in the same daily practice, and thus strive at an amendment of their faults. Those are mistaken in the honor which they would pay to this sacrament, when through respect, they but rarely receive it. S. Chrysostom confutes and condemns them."

After having shown, in eleven articles, the tradition of the fathers and of the councils on this subject, he concludes: "Behold the church which at all times, is the same, ever true and invariable in the purity of her doctrine, and unsusceptible of decay from any series of ages. The same spirit which guided and animated her, when in her bosom she nursed S. Justin and other holy men, directs and impels her now to hold the same language: to this day her exhortations to all her children towards FREQUENT communion, are equally pressing and spirited. The Christians, in former times of persecution, communicated in their own houses, and with their own hands, that they might not be deprived of DAILY communion. These latter times are not less dangerous and insidious; our common enemy is always awake, and aims at seduction by the venom of pride and luxury. Refined irreligion, pleasing and insinuating illusions, and deep hypocrisy, which, cancer-like, widely diffuse themselves, are more formidable obstacles to virtue, than racks and tortures.

Communicate therefore, as the apostles made the primitive Christians communicate, and as the fathers of the church caused to communicate the faithful of succeeding ages. Let those talk as they please, who are ever upon the reform, as to you, continue to eat this DAILY bread. Take your information and form your judgment, not from a set of pretended Reformers, who are always taking scandal at, and laboring at criticism on every subject, but from your lawful pastors, and from a discreet experienced director, who will lead you to the sense and meaning of the church, and guide you in the path in which formerly walked the best and wisest of your forefathers."

Can we therefore hesitate any longer to assert that, the doctors of every school, age, and country, who were in any degree eminent for their piety and learning, have methodically entered upon, and invincibly proved the excellency and advantage of **Frequent Communion?**

CHAPTER VII.

DECISIONS OF GENERAL AND PARTICULAR COUNCILS ON FREQUENT COMMUNION.

It must be allowed that every individual, though endowed with the keenest penetration, the greatest erudition, and the purest intentions, may possibly be mistaken in his decisions, and go astray in his judgment. We therefore stand in need of a living infallible guide, who, incapable of being deceived, as well as of deceiving, should banish, by his supreme authority, every doubt, remove every difficulty, and ultimately fix our fluctuating minds on what he decisively determines to be the truth. The discovery of a guide like this, is the business of the present moment.

Holy scripture no doubt is the written word of God, but being, what is called, a dead word, it does not, and cannot explain itself. There is therefore a necessity for an infallible living interpreter, whose unerring knowledge should mark and direct the true and real sense of it.

Tradition, the unwritten word of God, demands in like manner an additional testimony of its having originated from above, which testimony, unless infallible, would prove ineffectual.

The unanimous opinion of doctors, although weighty and persuasive, yields not however that absolute and perfect satisfaction, to which the human mind naturally inclines, and in which it strongly wishes finally to acquiesce. They are in the cause of religion, like able and eminent lawyers in civil debates, they are not judges, at least not infallible in their decisions. They may with the utmost propriety give advice, which, in general, to oppose, would be rash and inconsiderate; but they cannot ultimately determine, or pronounce a definite sentence. This singular and eminent prerogative is peculiar to the Church of Christ, composed of her leading pastors, in concert with the Pope at their head; for Jesus Christ has invested them, and them alone, with the unerring faculty and power of teaching all truth: *Go*, he says to his apostles[*], and in them to their successors, *go teach ye all nations, he that believeth shall be saved, he that believeth not shall be condemned.* I will send you

---

[*] Matth. xxviii. 19. Mark, xvi. 16. John xiv. 13. Matth. xviii. 20 Ibid. xviii. 17.

the Holy Ghost, *who will teach you all truth,* and behold, *I am with you all days, even to the consummation of the world.* He that doth not hear the church, let him be to thee as the heathen and the publican.

From which we are to infer, that a promise is here made of an absolute and independent infallibility, and that we are to listen to Christ's church, as to Christ himself : *he *that heareth you heareth me.* That it is a sovereign infallibility ; our salvation rests on our belief, the want of which seals our condemnation. That it is an universal infallibility extending to all religious matters, *all truth.* That it is a continued and an uninterrupted infallibility, *I am with you all days;* that it is a perpetual infallibility, *to the consummation of the world.* The church is founded on a solid rock, *and the powers of hell shall not prevail against it.* The church therefore, is that supreme and sovereign tribunal, which Jesus Christ has established to decide and determine, with absolute and infallible authority, all points of religious worship, of which it is he who speaks, as often as his church speaks ; let us now examine the decision of this church, in relation to Frequent Communion.

---

* Luke x. 16.

In the decree of the Council of Trent, at the beginning of the thirteenth session, we cannot but admire the awful majesty with which this assembled church enters upon the subject, and the becoming dignity which she assumes as the mother and mistress of all churches.

"The most holy and general council of Trent, peculiarly convened through the influence of the Holy Ghost, and presided over by the legate and nuncios of the holy apostolic see, although assembled with the view to explain the true and ancient doctrine on faith and on the sacraments, and to apply a proper remedy against all heresies ....has however, all along, paid particular attention to the extirpation of the cockle of those schisms and errors which the enemy has oversowed on the doctrine, the USE and on the worship of the holy Eucharist, which our Lord has left to his Church, as the symbol of union and of charity.

Wherefore the said holy council transmitting and teaching the same sound and pure doctrine, concerning the venerable sacrament of the Eucharist, which the Church, ever Catholic, has learned from the mouth of Jesus Christ, and of his apostles, and which she continues to learn from the Holy Ghost, who daily teaches her all truth, which truth she preserves, and will continue to preserve to the end of the world; this same council forbids and prohibits among the faithful, both teaching and preaching on the most holy Eucharist in any other manner, than is explained and defined in the present decree." In the eighth chapter of the above mentioned edition, the title of which is, *On the Use of the most admirable Sacrament of the Eucharist,* we read: "This holy council, with a truly paternal affection, admonishes, exhorts, entreats, and, through the bowels of God's mercy, conjures all and every one of those who bear the name of Christian, finally to unite in the bonds of charity, and being constantly mindful of the infinite majesty, and extreme love of Jesus Christ, who has given his life in ransom for our salvation, together with his flesh for our food, they would believe and reverence these sacred mysteries of his body and blood with such steadiness and firmness of faith, such devotion, piety and religious comportment, as may induce and dispose them FREQUENTLY to receive this bread, which is above all substance, that it may truly become the life of their soul, and the continual fervor of their mind, and thus strengthened and invigorated, they may safely pass through the temptations of this earthly pilgrimage, to the repose of their heavenly country."

From which words I infer, that the meaning of the council is, to persuade all in general, and every one in particular, to frequent communion : that frequent communion is held out as a sign of our being Christians, and pointed at as the fairest symbol of our union and charity : and that the infinite majesty and excessive love of Jesus Christ, should so impress the mind of every Christian, as to move and entice him to communicate often. The idea therefore of supreme Majesty, is not, in the opinion of the council, to withhold us from, but draw us to communion. And lastly, that frequent communion should be the result of the firmness of our faith, the fruit of our piety, and the effect of our religion, from whence shall flow spiritual life, preserved and invigorated with every help, suitable and conducive to the possession of that happy state, where we shall behold unveiled, and face to face, the now hidden object of our adoration, and the life-giving manna of our souls.

In the second chapter of the same decree, the said council makes use of three particular expressions, the obvious meaning of which, favors, in the clearest manner, even daily communion. "Our Lord, upon leaving this world, to return to his

Father, instituted this sacrament, in which he has wonderfully displayed the treasures of his divine love for man, and in the reception of it, he has commanded that his memory should be honored, and his death continually announced until he comes to judge mankind." Now as this command is always in force, and is uninterruptedly to be complied with, it consequently follows, that communion also must be uninterrupted, and of course, should be daily. The council adds, "That this sacrament should be considered as the spiritual food and strength of our souls." And we know that food and refreshment must be taken daily. Lastly in the opinion of the council, "This sacrament is to be received as an antidote which at once frees us from daily commissions, and preserves us against grevious offences."* Now a remedy like this, should doubtless be daily, because our slight transgressions being daily, we stand in need of a repeated forgiveness, and our misery is such, that we are in daily want of a powerful preservative from more weighty commissions. And elsewhere, "The sacred council could wish that, in every mass, at

---

* Sumi autem voluit sacramentum hoc tanquam spiritualium animorum cibum, quo alantur et consortentur: et tanquam antidotum quo liberemur a culpis quotidianis, et peccatis mortalibus preservemur. c. 2. sess. 13.

which the faithful assisted, they all did communicate, not only spiritually and in desire, but also really by a sacramental reception, the advantages of which would be more copious and lasting." †

Perfectly consonant with the sense of the universal Church was St. Charles Boromeo, in the provincial councils, which, on different occasions, he held at Milan. He speaks thus, "*Let curates and preachers, incessantly exhort the faithful to the most salutary custom of FREQUENTLY receiving the holy Eucharist, urging the example and practice of the primitive Church, the words and testimony of the holy fathers, and the unanimous sense of the sacred council of Trent, who recommends communion at every mass: and should any preacher, either directly or indirectly, advance an opinion which might take from, oppose, or invalidate this doctrine, the bishops of the town or diocese of the delinquent, must interdict him as a sower of scandal, and an opposer of the authority of the council of Trent." And in the first council of Milan, he had said before; "Let curates, by their repeated exhortations, strenuously labor that

---

† Optaret sancta Synodus ut in singulis Missis fideles adstantes non solum spirituali affectu, sed sacramentali etiam Eucharistiæ perceptione communicarent. c. 6. sess. 22.
* Council. Medial. c. 3. a. 7. De Eucharist.

the faithful, entrusted to their care, may FREQUENTLY go to confession and to communion." We read also in the fourth council, "Let every curate, both by exhorting his parishioners to frequent the sacraments, and by repeated instructions and admonitions, endeavor to renew the custom established by Pope St. Silverius, importing that, those who in the course of a year, do not communicate OFTEN, shall receive every Sunday, during Advent and Lent, the body of Jesus Christ." And lower down: "When communion is distributed to a concourse of people; the bishops, either in person, or by the help of others, are to be particularly attentive that the faithful, at that favorable juncture, be properly animated to fervor and devotion, by frequent and fervid acts of virtue, and by pathetic exhortations, which, like so many fiery darts, may spirit them on to FREQUENT communion. Let them also be made sensible how dangerous and pernicious it is to receive it unworthily, and yet how profitable, if worthily, to communicate OFTEN. Lastly, let no curate deprive the sick, who should desire it, of FREQUENT communion although they should not be in danger of death; the comfort arising from a repetition of this heavenly food is too great, and the emoluments accruing from it, are by far too desirable, to authorize a non-compliance on the part of the pastor."

We find in the council of Rheims, which was held in 1583, "As the Christian religion contains nothing that is equal in dignity and excellence to the most adorable sacrament of the Eucharist, and as there is nothing so efficaciously conducive to a virtuous and holy life, as a MOST FREQUENT participation of this heavenly banquet, it is a motive of grief and anguish to us to find that such, in these days, is the negligence and inattention of Christians, as to content themselves with a bare annual assistance from this most salutary sacrament. Let curates therefore, and preachers, strongly inculcate the ancient and commendable custom of FREQUENT communion; let them enlarge upon and display the most admirable fruits and innumerable advantages, which inevitably must flow from it; in fine, let them exert every power of speech, to persuade their flock, that there are no means better calculated, no method more compendious to quell and even extinguish the raging fire of heresy, and universally to revive, throughout the Christian world, the purity of religion, the fervid zeal, and every endearing virtue of primitive times." And farther on: "We also exhort all the faithful, and conjure them, through the bowels of God's great mercy, to communicate as OFTEN as it lies in their power, especially on solemn and festival days, and whenever any pressing necessity shall make it expedient."

In the year 1590, a council was held at Toulouse; in which we read : * The curates, preachers, and directors must persuade the faithful, by means of repeated exhortations, to MOST FREQUENT communion." And in 1624, the bishops of the council of Bordeaux say: "† We wish most ardently, that the faithful communicated MOST FREQUENTLY; and that, with the greatest devotion."

From the preceeding quotations I conclude, that the congregated fathers of the above councils express, in the strongest terms, their esteem for frequent communion, and their eagerness for establishing and preserving it. In their language, it is the great treasure of our holy religion: it is the best and shortest road to the practice of every virtue, it extirpates heresy, and the efficacy of it is such, as would infallibly renew those days of primitive fervor, which the apostles once formed and perfected. Nor are their exhortations con-

---

* Concil. Tolos. c. 5. de Euchar.
† Concil. Burdigal. c. 5. a. 3. de Euchar.

fined to a few in the Christian world: they speak to all and every one of that denomination, and they most pressingly invite and persuade all to MOST FREQUENT communion.

CHAPTER VIII.

DECISIONS AND REGULATIONS OF SOVEREIGN PONTIFFS, THROUGH A SUCCESSION OF AGES, CONCERNING FREQUENT COMMUNION.

Our Lord made a promise to Peter, that no deficiency should attend his faith; that it should become his charge to confirm his brethren in the faith; that the infant Church should be erected on Peter, who should teach no other doctrine than that of his Master. We are now going to see that the apostolical tradition, relative to frequent communion, has been uninterruptedly and invariably handed down to us in a long succession of many ages; we shall hear the mother and mistress of all churches, at the example of her heavenly spouse, loudly proclaiming, and cogently enforcing daily, or at least, most frequent communion : all the sovereign pontiffs shall speak on the occasion, and their unanimous voice, which has spread itself to the remotest parts of the globe, in favor of this subject, will be a confirmation to our faith, when we behold, that the living oracles of religious matters, the common fathers of the faithful, the visible heads of the church, and the vicars of Jesus Christ, have sufficiently spoken on frequent communion in the language of their divine Master.

St. Peter, in the same words, in which he acknowledged the divinity of the Son of God, acknowledged also that he admitted the doctrine concerning the frequent use of the blessed Eucharist, which he believed to be productive of life and immortality : for when our Redeemer had miraculously multiplied the five loaves, and had declared that he would give to the world a bread from heaven, which should be his own flesh as their food and nourishment, several of his desciples, taking offence, retired and left him. Jesus then, addressing his twelve desciples, asked, * *Will you also go away? Lord,* answered Simon Peter in the name of all, *to whom shall we go, thou hast the words of*

---

* John vi. 68.

eternal life. That is, in the interpretation of St. Augustin,† life everlasting is only attainable by a belief in your words: we believe all you have delivered to us concerning this heavenly food, we acknowledge your wisdom and power with which you can place your body in the Eucharist, and trust in your goodness, that you will make it our nourishment. It was upon this occasion, that Peter, for the first time, declared to his Master, and to all then present, that he would undertake to preach the doctrine of the Eucharist, and that, as head pastor, he would, with this food, feed the lambs and the sheep, which Jesus Christ was to commit to his care. He entered upon this function immediately after the descent of the Holy Ghost: and the first lesson he read to the newly baptised Christians, was to teach them the expediency of daily communion. They were persevering in the doctrine of the apostles, and in the communication of the breaking of bread, which was their daily custom.*

S. Anacletus, the fifth Pope from S. Peter, writes in his letter to the bishops of Italy: "After consecration, let all communicate; and those who re-

---

† Aug. Tract. 27. in Joan. * Acts, ii. 42.

fuse compliance, let them be forbidden the church for such is the apostolic statute, and such is the doctrine of the holy Roman church.†"

Although from the earliest period of the church frequent communion had been strictly enjoined by apostolical mandate, including excommunication on the transgressors; it was found, in course of time, that this primitive fervor relented among some Christians, whilst among others the obligation itself was, either falling into oblivion, or was totally neglected. To obviate so great an evil, Pope St. Fabian determined and reduced the above precept to three different periods in the year, Easter, Whitsuntide and Christmas, yet warmly exhorting and strongly soliciting every one of the faithful to present himself much more frequently at the sacred table, than the three mentioned times of obligatory communion—St Soter added Maunday Thursday.

But as charity among several still continued on the decline, and as there were Christians to be found, who for years had absented themselves from communion, Innocent III confined the obligation

---

† Peracta consecratione, omnes communicent; qui noluerint, cclesiasticis carere liminibus: sic enim apostoli statuerunt, et sancta Romana tenet ecclesia. Quem citat S. Thom. 3. p. q. 80. a. 10.

of it to Easter, annexing on the delinquents expulsion from the church during their lifetime, and privation of Christian burial at their death.*

From these pontifical ordinances it cannot be inferred that frequent communion was then in the least opposed, or not approved of : on the contrary, those pious pontiffs greatly wished for it, and even supposed that every good Christian communicated often. The words, *if not oftener, at least* once in the year, sufficiently show their meaning. The question no ways related to frequent Communion, but solely to unfrequent communions, at which they grieved, and against which they thundered out the severest excommunication.

During the first five centuries, St. Jerome and St. Augustine inform us, that the faithful communicated daily, not only with the knowledge and approbation, but also through the exhortations of sovereign pontiffs. Their chief solicitude was to feed their flock with this heavenly nourishment ; the strongest persecutions did not abate their zeal on this head ; and if the rage of their enemies prevented their pious assemblies during the day, the night favored their devotion in subterraneous

---

* Concil. Later. Sess. 13.

vaults, where mass was constantly celebrated, and communion carefully distributed. S. Stephen Pope, let no day pass without offering the immaculate lamb, and was gifted with the palm of martyrdom, while actually engaged in that most sacred of all functions. We know from ecclesiastical history, that all the Popes of the first five centuries, most of whom were also martyrs, ordained many bishops and priests, with the view to multiply every where the sacrifice of the altar, and to facilitate the distribution of the Eucharist in every part of the Christian world.

In the fifth age, Gelasius Pope, composed hymns, prefaces and prayers, which were to be said at the sacrifice of the mass, and in the administration of the sacraments. The same Gelasius was the first who formed a sacramentary, in which the offices and ceremonies appertaining to the mass for every day in the year, are carefully regulated, and vary but little from the method which is actually now in use. It is therefore plain that his meaning was to favor daily communion at least among priests, nor can it be supposed that the laity were excluded from this daily blessing, since it has been observed elsewhere, yet cannot be too often repeated, that in those days, the faithful seldom or never assisted at the sacrifice without receiving the sacrament.

In the same century, Leo the great, and the first Pope of the name, communicated, say Valfridus and Durandus, from seven to nine times every day*. The zeal of this pontiff, though great in building or repairing churches to God's Honor, was still greater and more active in supporting frequent communion : of this he gives proof in his letter to the bishops of Vienna : "Communion should not easily be refused to any of the faithful, nor should the refusal of it promiscuously depend on the caprice of every priest whose zeal for purity of conscience may be exclusive, and wound up to too stern a degree of rigorism : we are informed that this has happened ; and that several have been deprived of the benefit of this sacrament, for the commission of some venial faults, or for the utterance of some unprofitable and idle words: it is not becoming that any soul, for whom the blood of Christ was shed, should undergo so unproportionable a punishment, because under such a privation she would be left destitute of proper help, and exposed defenceless to the wiles of her enemy,

---

*Vais, in l. de rebus eccles. Durand. in rationali D. Office l. 4. c. 1.

whose craft, in this her weakness, would easily circumvent her§."

In the sixth century, Gregory the Great, writes to his friend Eulogium, "We celebrate mass daily, in which we commemorate the holy martyrs." In his eighth letter, he says: "I have now been confined to bed through the gout, for near two years: and my pains are so acute, that I can hardly celebrate on holydays." In his book on sacramental matters, which regulates the masses for every day in the year, this pontiff clearly shows his zeal for frequent communion, when he says†: "The Lord is taken DAILY, that we may obtain pardon of our daily transgressions." And elsewhere we read*: "We should despise from our hearts this present world, because it is but momentary: whilst our whole employ should be to make an offering to God of our tears, and DAILY to immolate the sacrifice of his flesh and blood."

Nicholas I. in the ninth article of his answer to the Bulgarians, says‡: "You may communicate EVERY DAY in Lent, as well as any other time: from which practice, we earnestly pray to the Almighty Lord that you may never depart, and to our prayers we sincerely add our warmest exhorta-

---

§ Ann. 598.   † Serm. 4. de Quadrag.   * Dial. l. 4. c. viii.   ‡ An. 866.

tions to the continuance of it." And in the thirty-fifth article, he recommends in lieu of their former superstitions in their preparations for war, that they would seek for better defence from an assiduity at the holy altars, and a frequent participation of the holy mysteries.

To render daily communion more easy and practicable, Pope Stephen, who lived in the same century, abolished the custom which had obtained in St. Peter's church, of exacting by way of license, a yearly sum of money from every priest, who to indulge his devotion, chose that place for his daily offerings. And Pope Leo the IX. who had been bishop of Toul, immolated the immaculate lamb every day of his life.

St. Gregory the VII. of that name, in his thirteenth letter to the princess Malthides, says: " Among the many arms, which, by the grace of God, I have pointed out to you, to shield you from the snares of the prince of this world, the chief and the most excellent, is frequently to receive the body of our Lord, and to place the greatest confidence in the protection of the mother of God."

St. Peter Celestian, relented twice from his custom of daily celebration, because some disagreeable temptations, indicated, as he thought, his unworthiness to receive so often; but our Lord, both by revelation, and by the advice of a holy man, made known to him, that his daily offerings were by far more pleasing, than his misplaced reverence and respect. It is therefore beyond a doubt, that through the course of the first thirteen centuries of the Church, the tradition and doctrine of soverign pontiffs, have invariably taught, supported, and favored frequent communion.

An additional and superabundent proof of what has been said, obviously presents itself from the institution of the feast in honor of this great sacrament, which took place under Urban the fourth. The bull, which this pontiff issued on the occasion, is an admirable compendium of the many wonders which flow from the eucharistic offering*. He admits, that it is frequently and even DAILY attended to, and received by the faithful, but yet wishes that, during this more solemn festival, all should particularly unite in praises and thanksgivings to God for so many unmerited blessings, and by their earnest and redoubled fervor, they would repair in some measure, the many injuries and

---

* Licet igitur hoc memoriale sacramentum in QUOTIDIANIS Missarum solemniis frequentetur, conveniens est . . . duximus statuendum ut de tanto sacramento præter QUOTIDIANAM memoriam quam de ipso facit Ecclesia, solemnior et specialior annuatim memoria celebretu. *Bulla* Transiturus.

insults which are yearly offered, by loose Christians, to this adorable sacrament. I could cite many other regulations and decrees, of several great and holy pontiffs, tending to encourage and promote frequent communion; but, to avoid prolixity, I content myself with observing, that the zeal of these heads of the Church, for this holy practice is very conspicuous in the number of monasteries and churches which they erected and founded, to extend the practice and facilitate the use of communion: in the number of pious missionaries, whom they have solicitously sent, and indefatigably send to this day, to all parts of the globe, to propagate the doctrine, and inculcate the utility of this wonderful sacrament; in the number of persons of both sexes, whose names they have classed in the list of saints, chiefly because they had drawn their sanctity from daily or frequent communion: in their approbation of many religious orders of men, whose duty it should be to spread the priesthood, and provide the faithful with preachers and directors, to instruct them in, and lead them to, the practice of holy communion: in the encouragement they have given to a variety of communities of women, and pious virgins, who consecrate their lives, by night and by day, in singing the praises of their heavenly spouse concealed in the Eucharist, and who, through a frequent and daily participation of his hidden treasures, emulate in love, and resemble in purity the spirits above: in the great number of confraternities established in honor of the blessed sacrament, which increasing under the approbation of the holy See, have extended themselves universally over the Christian world: in the grant of many indulgences, which include, as a necessary condition, holy communion: and finally, in the number of general as well as provincial councils, which they have assembled and confirmed for the refutation of those heretics, who, by broaching various errors, have impugned this inestimable sacrament: thus Beringarius stood condemned by Leo IX. and again by Nicholas II. and thirdly by Gregory VII. Wickliff also and John Hus, by Leo X. Paul III. Jules III. and Pius IV. who, in their confirmation of the council of Trent, declare, enjoin, and order that whatever has been regulated and defined, either relative to the real presence of Jesus Christ in the Eucharist, or to the frequent use of this sacrament, must be inviolably observed by all and every one of the faithful: lastly, many errors contained in several books, tending to deter, and withdraw from frequent communion, have received condemnation from Innocent X, Alexander VII. and several other popes down to the present time.

We read in the catechism of the council of Trent, published by order of Pius V. *"It is incumbent on curates, frequently to inculcate on the minds of their flock, that as they take DAILY corporal nourishment, they also should be particularly careful DAILY to feed their souls with the blessed Eucharist: the manna, which was the figure of the eucharistic bread, was the DAILY food of the Children of Israel. We are not therefore to imagine, that St. Augustine was particular in his opinion, when he said, *You sin daily, and therefore communicate daily:* it is the universal and unanimous sense of the fathers." The said pope celebrated mass every day; and indulged Mary queen of Scots, during her rigorous confinement, in receiving at pleasure, the consecrated bread, which had been secretly brought to her.

Innocent XI, in one of his bulls, speaks in the following manner: "Although the frequent and daily use of the holy Eucharist, has always been

---

* Cat. Con. Frid. 2. p. c. 4. sess. 60.

approved of by the most holy fathers of the church*, they have not exactly determined the particular days, either of the month or week on which the faithful were to receive it: even the council of Trent, has not specified them: this holy council however, having in view the frailty of fallen man, has clearly signified the warmest wishes and desires for frequent communion, and judiciously has avoided the nomination of fixed times for this holy duty. For as the human eye cannot penetrate the foldings of the heart, nor human prudence discern the degree of dissipation to which many of the faithful may be subject in their various occupations, nor yet discover the graces and gifts which God imparts to his children, so no general rule or order can be given, which determines the proper disposition, and exact purity of heart of each particular penitent, with respect to FREQUENT and DAILY communion.

It is therefore necessary, that this business should be left to directors, whose prudence is to mark out the safest path to their respective penitents: when and how often merchants and married people should receive communion, as it shall seem

---

* Etsi frequens quotidianusque sanctæ Eucharistiæ usus a sanctissimis Patribus fuerit in Ecclesia semper probatus. Bulla Innoc. XI.

beneficial to them, suitable to the purity of their souls, and proportionable to the fruits they reap from it. The principal care therefore and concern of bishops, must be by no means to withdraw or terrify souls from FREQUENT or DAILY communion, but to encourage and prompt them to it, as it suits their devotion, or as it is conformable to the opinion of their pastors and directors. Bishops also must see that no one be withheld from this heavenly banquet, even though they should desire to assist at it DAILY: but whether it be sought for seldom or often, each particular penitent must be allowed full liberty to taste of that divine sweetness, which is imparted to him in proportion to his devotion and purity of heart. It is also to be published, that those religious women, who, besides the days assigned by their rule, are judged fit to receive *oftener*, and even *daily*, are by no means to be impeded by their superiors. To the endeavors of pastors and directors, it is extremely proper and desirable, that preachers also should join their assistance, in moving and exciting the faithful to FREQUENT communion; this is a duty no less incumbent on them, than that of teaching their hearers what preparations and dispositions are requisite for so holy an action."

From the preceding positions I draw the following obvious conclusions: FREQUENT, and even DAILY communication has always been approved of by the fathers of the Church. The Church has never singled out any particular days for going to, or abstaining from communion, but has left it to the discretion of every faithful soul, under the guidance of an approved director. It is not to priests only, or to religious persons, that frequent and daily communion is recommended or allowed; the above mentioned decree, invests with the same privilege the laity, merchants, and married people. The bishops are not to withdraw from, but by every means to excite the faithful to frequent communion: and though preachers are put in mind to inspire their congregations with the greatest reverence for the holy Eucharist, they are never to discourage frequent and even daily communion: a proper respect for this sacrament, a just dread of sin, can never be sufficiently inculcated, but this awe and respect must tend to enforce to draw and lead to frequent communion. Such is the constant and invariable doctrine of all those pontiffs who have successively filled the chair of St. Peter: and such has ever been the uniform doctrine of the Church of God.

CHAPTER IX.

THE OPINION AND PRACTICE OF THE SAINTS CONCERNING FREQUENT COMMUNION.

The authority of the fathers, doctors, councils and sovereign pontiffs, has hitherto been the means made use of to throw light on, and even to decide the important question in hand: and as they have an indisputed right to be considered as our teachers and judges in all religious matters, to oppose or prevent their doctrine in favor of frequent communion, would betray great ignorance, or what is still worse, a great depravity of heart. Frequent and daily communion, is, as we have proved, the tenet of the doctors, it is also that of the saints of Christ's Church: and as their example and sentiments, relative to communion, must be supposed to have been truly pure and heavenly, a fair exposition of what they did and thought, must carry conviction to the mind of every impartial reader.

Some of our modern reformers, have either ignorantly or maliciously maintained, that several of the saints have opposed frequent communion:

and that others, from a sense of self unworthiness, have refrained from it, by way of better preparation for some future time. But if it be true that the intention of Jesus Christ and that of his church has an opposite tendency, if the doctrine of the fathers during the first ten or twelve centuries enforce the contrary practice, it evidently follows, that either these assertions are groundless and false, or that this peculiar conduct of such saints, was no ingredient of their sancity: and we know that some mistaken anchorets were severely reprimanded by St. Chrysostom for the unfrequency of their communions.

There are others again, who assert, that the recluses who dwelt in Egypt, as well as in other countries, communicated but seldom, first, they say, because they had no opportunity so to do, and second, because we read nothing concerning it in their lives. Plausible as the position may seem to be, I hope amply to satisfy the reader, that those holy solitaries, both of the east and west part of the globe, had opportunities of commnnion, and availed themselves of them daily.

If we go back to the fourth century, in which period the deserts flourished with Anthonies, Pacomiuses and other illustrious leaders of numberless monks, who then peopled the eastern recesses, we shall learn that the recluses of those happy days resorted from time to time to the Christian town assemblies, where they joined the faithful in communion, and on their return took with them the blessed Eucharist, of which they partook, when alone in their cells. This truth is attested by St. Jerome and St. Chrysostom: and St. Basil informs us that such was the practice of the recluses he lived with. The following are his words:

"To communicate EVERY DAY, and to receive the sacred body of Jesus Christ, is most commendable and salutary: as to us, we communicate four times in the week, Sundays, Wednesdays, Fridays and Saturdays, and on other days also, when there intervenes a festival either of our Lord or of a saint. In times of persecutions, each one, when destitute of priest and clerk communicates himself. ALL THOSE who lead an eremetical life, where no priest is at hand*, keep by them the blessed Eucharist and receive it. In Alexandria, and in Egypt, even the most part of the laity, follow this

---

* Omnes qui in eremo sunt, ubi non est sacerdos, communionem domi habentes accipiunt. In Alexandria et Egypto unusquisque ex iis qui ex populo sunt, ut plurimum communionem domi habentes, cum vult, assumit.
       Basil. ad patri. Cæsar. c. ult.

practice, and communicate themselves, as their devotion suggests."

The disciples of the renowned Pacomius†, on the return of every festival, sent for a priest from the neighboring villages, to celebrate and distribute the sacred mysteries; which, when they received, their custom was to lay aside their cloak and girdle, retaining only their cassock. In process of time, Pacomius fixed a priest in every monastery.

Cassian informs us, that the hermit Paphnutius, even when four score and ten years of age, regularly walked to a church six miles off, every Saturday and Sunday, where he said mass to the monks of Scetis, and gave them communion*. In the town of Oxiringa, situated in the Lower Thebes‡, there were in different convents and monasteries twenty thousand virgins, and ten thousand monks: the number of their churches amounted to twelve, besides several oratories belonging to the monks, where mass and communion were constantly performed.

Not far from a town called Antinous, there flourished ten convents of women, who resorted every Sunday to a neighboring church, to partake

---

† A. D. 363. 1. 2. Hist. Fleury. * Cass. Col. 3. c. i. ‡ Pallad. Vit. Pat. 2. c. v.

of the holy mysteries. And in the desert of Nitria, for the same pious purpose, eight priests belonged to one church, which was frequented by five thousand monks, who lived in fifty adjoining monasteries*.

Near the town of Hermopolis, which stood on the banks of the river Nile, where it is believed that the Virgin mother and St. Joseph had carried the Infant Jesus in their flight into Egypt, there were assembled five thousand monks, under the direction of the great Appollonius, whose constant endeavor it was to promote daily communion: he was ever apprehensive lest an estrangement from this sacrament should bring on a neglect of every other duty. He was also particularly attentive, that none of his followers should breakfast before that holy action‡.

St. Luke, junior, a famous solitary†, upon hearing that the archbishop of Corinthia was to pass by the mountain of St. John, went thither to give him the greeting, and presented him with a few herbs which his little garden afforded. The prelate, pleased with the gift, would take a view of

---

* Pallad. c. cxxxvii.   ‡ Vitæ Pat. Appol.   † Boland. Febr.
T. 4. p. 83.

his habitation, and in return, tendered to him some pieces of gold. But the holy man refusing the offer, said, it is not gold I want; all I stand in need of are prayers and instructions: however, to remove the chagrin which he perceived his refusal had occasioned, he took one piece of money, and continued his discourse; *my Lord, we whom our sins have driven into deserts, no priest within reach of us, by what means are we to partake of the holy mysteries?* The archbishop replied, you must do what you can to procure one, and if your endeavors prove unsuccessful, you will place the vase of consecrated bread on the altar, if you make use of an oratory, or else, if in your cell, you will take a clean table, and spread over it a cloth, on which you will put the sacred host; you will then sing the *Trisagion*, or the hymn which names God three times holy, to which you will add the creed, and after three genuflections, you will take with your mouth the body of Jesus Christ.

St. Sabas, inhabitant of Syria, abbot of several monasteries, renowned throughout the East, for the austerity of his life, and respected by several emperors, for his irreproachable conduct, never took any nourishment during Lent, but what he received from the Eucharistic bread.

It is not therefore a point to be held questionable, whether frequent communion universally prevailed among the recluses of the East, the facts which I have alleged, prove it beyond a doubt: and as the monastic mode of living was transferred from East to West, it is equally unquestionable, that the same spirit diffused itself among the monks of the western climates. This however, is what we shall now investigate, trusting that the bare investigation alone, will dissipate every objection that can be made to the contrary.

It is advanced by some, that St. Benedict, the patriarch of western recluses, lay concealed a long while in his retreat without communicating: that he founded twelve menasteries on, or near the mountain Cassinus, and that in the rules which he laid down for their observance, no mention is made of communion. The fallacy of this way of reasoning, I should think is too glaring, not to be observed by an impartial eye. This saint, it is true, was three years concealed from the knowledge of all mankind, exclusive of one single monk, whose name was Roman: and as this faithful friend provided him with corporal nourishment, it is obvious to conclude that he was still more his friend in his spiritual concerns, by supplying him with the

Eucharist, which practice, we have observed, was frequent among recluses.

It is a known fact, that the anchorets of the west as well as of the east, either resorted to public meetings in town or country, or had priests to come to them, from whom they received communion: and when they went out, if they had no priest in community, they took home with them the blessed Eucharist.

Guimundus, bishop of Aversa, in the kingdom of Naples, writes*, that the ancient hermits were in general so comforted and invigorated by communion, that several of them took no other nourishment: and that if at any time they chanced to abstain from this heavenly table, they perceptibly flagged in spirits and in health. He adds, that many of those holy men communicated daily, through the ministry of angels.

If the primitive rule of St. Benedict makes no mention of frequent communion, this silence must have proceeded from the prevailing custom among Christians in general of frequent communion; it would therefore have been needless to recommend that to religious people, which even among the laity was held as a point of duty.

---

* Tract. de Corp. et Sang. Jes. Christ. in Euch. veritate.

St. Gregory confirms my assertion: this great prelate, not long after the death of St. Bennet, charmed with the excellency of his rules, embraced the monastic state, and in time was chosen abbot; no day passed which he did not sanctify by celebrating mass, and he inspired the communities of the seven monasteries, which he built, with the same devotion: and when Pope, the better to promote this holy practice, he appointed priests for every monastery, exempted the Italian monks from episcopal jurisdiction, and freed them from the obligation of resorting to public meetings.

This pontiff, whose zeal was indefatigable, sent St. Augustine with apostolic power to the happy island of Great Britain, where the christian faith, the monastic life, and frequent communion soon became so conspicuous, as to attract the admiration of the rest of the Christian world. History furnishes us with a particular proof of what I advance. One Theodore had ruled the abbey of Cromall for the space of sixty-two years: when the Normans made an irruption, which threatened the monastery with plunder and destruction. The venerable abbot ordered thirty of his monks, ten of whom were priests, to retire elsewhere: meanwhile, the consecrated plate, and an elegant and costly table belonging to the high altar, were concealed in a deep well. Theodore and the remaining monks went in their church robes to the choir, sung as usual their canonical hours, the abbot celebrated high mass, and gave communion to all who were present. By this time, the barbarians had forced their way into the church, one of their kings, by name Osketul, slew the abbot on the altar, whilst his attendants beheaded the assisting ministers.

About the same time,[*] Grimlaic gave to the anchorets in England the following rule: "The recluses shall shut themselves up in a cell, and shall make a vow never to go out of it: the cells shall adjoin to a monastery, they shall be small and carefully closed up, and provided with everything necessary. If the recluse be a priest, he must have an oratory consecrated by a bishop, and a window must face the Church, through which he is to take his offerings for mass." He also strongly recommends mental prayer, and greatly approves of daily mass and communion[†].

The order of Cluni was formed in the tenth century, much upon the plan of that of St. Bene-

---

[*] A. D. 893.   [†] C. 36. Cod. Reg. T. 2. p. 464.

dict. Ulric, a member of that community, informs us, that "the monks of Cluni sung two high masses on all festival days, one of the day, and the other for the dead: one side of the choir communicated on the three first days of the week, and the other side on the other three: in time of divine office, several low masses were offered†."

We read in the life of St. Odilon, one of the first abbots of the said order, that he celebrated mass daily, for the space of fifty-six years: and on his deathbed he entreated one of his monks, Abraldus, to sum up the number of masses which he had said throughout his life, as if the reward which he was in immediate expectation of, depended on his assiduity in this holy practice. Near the same time, Cardinal Matthew, who had also been a member of that order, never retrenched any part of the long psalmody he had been used to, and always persevered in his daily offering.

Richard, abbot of St. Vanne, and a follower of the Benedictine rule, conducted to Jerusalem, at his own expense, seven hundred pilgrims: during his journey, he recited the divine office, and celebrated mass daily: even when on infidel ground,

---

†A. D. 1391.

and surrounded by heathens, he did not omit the holy offering—and frequently performed his devotion at a little distance from their towns, whilst they were insulting him from their walls with volleys of stones, and shouts of derision—Providence protected him from mischief, and his patience bore with their mockeries.

St. Bruno, founder of the Carthusian order, so justly famed for holy retirement, was particularly attentive to frequent communion. For according to their constitutions, which were collected by Guigne, one of their first generals, these virtuous men are enjoined confession either to their prior, or to some one deputed for that purpose, on Saturdays; and Sundays a mass was celebrated, besides the conventual offering. In their churches there was nothing of gold or of silver, except a chalice and a tube through which they received the sacred blood. They therefore communicated at least weekly, from the first formation of their holy institution.

The stern and severe discipline of the hermits of Camaldoli, was first planned by St. Romuald: singular was the austerity of his life; and as singular was the height of perfection to which he attained. Besides his foresight into things to come, he was raised to a contemplation, which was animated with seraphic love, and which frequently forced from him these emphatic words, "Dear Jesus, my sweet Jesus, my ineffable desire!" He daily said mass, though not in public, on account of a constant flood of tears which his devotion drew from him. The irregular conduct of one of his monks, having obliged him to reprove him severely, the unhappy delinquent took his revenge by recrimination. The calmuny, for a while, gained credit, though the virtue of the abbot was upheld by many miracles, and strongly supported by the venerable sanction of old age. His disciples condemned him to particular penances, and suspended him from the holy sacrifice. The humility of the saint made him acquiesce in silence for the space of six months, to the rigor of the sentence; after which, our Lord appeared to him and bade him lay aside his indiscreet simplicity, and as usual to celebrate mass: the next day he obeyed, and during the sacrifice, he remained for a considerable time enraptured.

From what has been said of St. Bernard, it is clear, that his monks communicated most frequently: and we have from himself, that numbers of other monks and abbots, followed the same custom:

he seldom or never omitted mass, to the last day of his life; and this same practice he had introduced into seventy-two monasteries, which he had either founded, or incorporated with his order.

St. Norbert, who also instituted a religious order, daily sacrificed the immaculate Lamb. Being engaged one day in this heavenly function, in a subterraneous chapel, a large spider dropped into the chalice after consecration. The respect and love with which his breast glowed, removed from it every shadow of fear of evil consequences, and therefore at the usual time, he swallowed what was contained in the cup, without concern. Mass being over, he entered upon his prayers of thanks, in some expectation of death: the event however was otherwise: and most probably he was miraculously preserved. This servant of God, sold all he was possessed of, except what was necessary for the holy sacrifice; which he frequently offered twice in the day.

I cannot omit mentioning the zeal of St. Fulgentius, bishop of Africa, not only for his own frequency of communion, but also for promoting the same devotion in several large and populous cities. *This great and admirable doctor, charmed

---
* 6 Century.

the age he lived in with the beauty of his genius, and the noble candor and sincerity of his heart. A considerable part of his life was monastic, and several monasteries, both in Africa and Sicily, acknowledged him for their founder. At length, being compelled to take up the episcopal dignity, he entered upon his functions by celebrating the holy mysteries, and distributing among his flock, their daily bread. He was sent from Africa into banishment, for the second time, by king Trasamont, of Arian principles: this prince was too impatient of the zeal of the saint, to behold with indifference the innumerable conversions which his indefatigable labors were continually effecting; but to conceal his departure, he ordered him to be shipped off in the night. The wind however being unfavorable to the king's intention, the ship, for several days, was confined to the coast. This gave the alarm, and spread among the Carthagenians, the fate of their beloved pastor. Almost the whole town assembled on the shore to take their leave of him; he received them with the tenderness of a father, exhorted them to virtue, and fed them all with the bread of life.

From the above general and constant tradition, it seems evident, that frequent communion was in force, both in the eastern and western deserts, in every age of the church: nor is it improper to observe, that, if we do not always read in the lives of saints, that they communicated, we never read any where that they did not communicate. Frequent communion was a common and ordinary practice among every set of Christians; and historians in general, transmit to posterity, facts only and occurrences, which are uncommon and extraordinary. Innumerable are the saints whose baptismal registers are no where recorded; are we therefore to conclude, that they were not baptized? How pitiful would the reasoning be that should urge, we have no account in history of the baptism of many saints, it was therefore the practice in their times to go without baptism, we therefore, at their example, may omit that sacrament? this parity will be allowed to be substantially deficient: for no point can warrantably be set up for imitation, that is not good in itself, conformable to the rules of Christ's Church, and clearly ascertained as an undoubted fact. Unfrequent communion is destitute of these three characters, whilst frequent communion has the full sanction of all three.

From the praise which our Redeemer bestowed on the humility of the Centurion, who said, "Lord

I am not worthy that thou shouldst come under my roof," some one may infer, that we may, with equal propriety, entertain the same sort of sentiment, and, by abstaining from communion, may deserve the same approbation both from Christ and his Church. But he who is biased to this way of reasoning, should first reflect, that neither Christ nor his Church, can ever approve of conduct which widely strays from their intention, and clearly opposes their express command. The Centurion, of whom the gospel speaks, knew no precept which obliged him to give our Lord admittance: and were communion equally at our option, were we equally unacquainted with our Savior's desire as he was, a resemblance of speech and sentiment in us, would be equally commendable.

There are others who oppose to this doctrine, the example of St. Bennet and St. Francis, who never could be prevailed upon to take priestly orders, while we read of some other saints, who, though in orders, were afraid to celebrate.

The character of priesthood is, doubtless, the most sacred and awful that can be assumed. It is a known truth, that many saints have refused holy orders: it is not every one who is called to that dignity: neither is there any law which enforces the acceptance of it: the point actually in question, relates not to priesthood, but to frequent communion, as enjoined by Jesus Christ and his Church: the humility of the above mentioned saints, was no obstacle to their frequent-communion, nor the least hindrance to their reading the same lesson to all their deciples.

If we read of a few holy men, who, though in orders, refrained from their privilege, we read at the same time, that they were reprimanded for their timidity and misplaced respect, and commanded to follow the more beaten track, of frequent offering: we have elsewhere observed, that this was the case with St. Peter Celestin: and a similar motive of humanity led St. Bonaventure into the same misunderstood devotion, till an angel came to communicate him, by which favor, he was readily brought to a daily participation of the heavenly banquet.

But, after all, it is not everything which every saint may have done, that claims our imitation; singly considered, they are men, and consequently fallible; they acknowledged their mistake, and came back to the living and unerring rule, which is the Church: whilst they moved according to doctrine and practice, they called on us to do as they did: but in no other supposition. The Church never has yet, and never will propose to our imitation the conduct of any saint whose maxim it might have been to abstain from frequent communion.

On the contrary this spouse of Jesus Christ, exhibits to our view and veneration, an endless string of martyrs, who by virtue of the eucharistic bread, became superior to the keenest torments, and triumphed over death itself. By means of the same heavenly manna, thousands of virgins, whom the church now honors, preserved in their mortal bodies, a purity equal to that of angels, which is the special and common effect of frequent communion*. From the same source the thrones of great kings and emperors drew sanctity and lustre: queens also and empresses graced their elevated station from the frequent participation of this hidden treasure; innumerable others of every age, rank, and condition, have, by the same means, arrived at the highest pitch of perfection, they are placed in the calendar of saints, their example is set before us, that we may do as they have done; the

---

* Vinum germinans virgines. Zach. 9.

catalogue is long, it would be endless to descend to every particular: yet for greater satisfaction, I shall briefly point out the practice and opinions of some holy men and women relative to this subject.

Thomas of Aquin, the brightest ornament of his respectable order, celebrated mass daily, and constantly assisted at a second, by way of thanksgiving. Peter Martyr, and Vincent Ferreri of the same religious body, and both conspicuous for their apostolic labors, regularly began the day with the holy offering, and were incessent panegyrists of frequent communion.

S. Catharine of Sienna, who was the wonder and prodigy of her sex for her angelical purity, her admirable patience and heavenly wisdom, habitually burned with the greatest desire of daily communion. She passed several Lents on no other food than the eucharistic bread. It once happened that her director refused to indulge her with communion, but he was soon made sensible of his indiscretion: for as he was celebrating mass, and being on the point of communicating, he only could find half of the sacred host, which threw him into the greatest perplexity and consternation, in which he continued, till mass being over, the holy virgin gave him comfort, by saying, set your mind at rest, the Lord has granted me what you had refused me: an angel has communicated me with that part of the host which occasioned your distress. From whence he took the lesson never more to thwart her pious desires. A certain bishop, whose opinion was rather unfavorable to this daily custom of Catherine, insinuated to her that weekly communion might be better, and alleged the saying of St. Augustine, importing that he neither approved or disapproved of daily communion, to which she replied, *do then as he did, if you do not approve of it, do not disapprove of it.*

S. Francis of Borgia, while duke of Candia, and viceroy of Catalona, fed weekly at the sacred table, which gave rise to an altercation among the Spanish doctors*. Some were of opinion that this frequency derogated from the respect which was due to so great a sacrament; others, on the contrary, strenuously supported the right which the viceroy had to tread in the footsteps of the primitive Christians, and to move in conformity to the authority of the fathers. The contention, for a time, was stubborn on both sides, but was happily

---

* Salmer. tract, 24. de frequent. usu Eucharist.

terminated by the interposition of S. Thomas of Villa Nova, who peremptorily decided in favor of frequent communion. Meanwhile the duke, for further satisfaction wrote to Ignatius of Loyola, who at that time was famous for the many illustrations with which heaven had favored him, entreating his opinion on the subject. The answer of the saint was: "That, in general, it was true to say, that one of the many good effects of frequent communion, is to help those that fall into imperfections through weakness and human frailty, speedily and easily to rise again: it is much more safe to receive this divine sacrament with love, reverence and confidence, than to keep from it through fear and timidity: and as the duke's way of life was regular and exemplary, he advised him by all means to continue his pious custom, not doubting that not only he himself would be greatly benefited by it, but others also, from his example." This kind of prophecy was amply fulfilled in course of time; Borgia, when viceroy and when a religious of the society of Jesus, was so successful in Spain and Portugal in promoting frequent communion, that both courts assumed the form of academies of virtue.

St. Francis Xavier, the apostle of the Indies,

had learned at the school of Ignatius to propagate with the greatest zeal this holy practice, and was so successful, that, in divers parts of the kingdom of Portugal, and particularly at the court of John III. then reigning, weekly communion became universal. He carried this doctrine to the Indies, which was powerful enough to sanctify millions of proselytes and other Christians. He daily began his apostolic functions with the holy mass, and through a veneration for this great sacrament, he always distributed it on his knees. Among the many wonders which the Indies beheld in this saint, that which made him appear in size above what was human, when he gave communion, was most striking and astonishing.

With these Christian heroes, I class St. Francis of Sales, the great apostle of Savoy and France, who brought back to the fold of Christ seventy-two thousand Calvinists; he speaks, as follows, of communion: "Mithridates king of Pontus, to guard against the effects of poison, had made familiar to himself a certain food which in course of time rendered him so robust, that, when on the point of being taken by the Romans, and in dread of slavery, he tried unsuccessfully the destructive bane. Is this not what the Lord has contrived in the Eucharist, in which he gives us his body, and his adorable blood as a food to which immortality is annexed*? Whoever therefore frequently and devoutly partakes of it, receives so much strength and vigor, that it is almost impossible for any deadly poison of sinful inclinations to affect his soul. No; a man cannot partake of this food of life, and die the death of sin. It would be an imprudence to advise everybody to DAILY COMMUNION, but it would be no less imprudent to dissuade every one from it, or blame DAILY COMMUNION: for several pious souls may be properly disposed for so great a blessing, and may be authorised by their directors so to do."

He answers every objection that can be made, and removes every difficulty, by saying: "And truly the primitive Christians communicated EVERY DAY, even those who were married; wherefore I advance the argument that FREQUENT communion can be no ways improper for any one."

In his introduction as well as in his letters, he warmly recommends frequent and daily communion; and the order of the visitation, which he formed on the model of the primitive church,

---

* Devout life on freq. commun. 2. p. c. xx.

clearly delineates his sentiments on this head. His whole plan and regulations seem to drive at this particular point, and those would be perfect followers of his rule, whose practice it was to receive daily.

The famous woman of mount Carmel, Teresa, during the three and twenty last years of her life, communicated daily: from that time she was freed from a retching, which till then she had been subject to every morning. She was often seen at her communions, surrounded with glory, and in her thanksgivings enraptured in the air.

There was nothing which she more pressingly recommended to the faithful than a due attention to avail themselves, to the best advantage, of those precious moments, during which Jesus Christ is in their breasts, before the consummation of the sacred species. What this saint writes on the fourth demand in the Lord's prayer, deserves particular notice.

"I cannot persuade myself, that the object of our petition to God in these words, *give us this day our daily bread,* is temporal to preserve the body: we entreat him to give us the most holy Eucharist, which is the bread above all substance, it is to pray that he himself should become our food." And lower down: "It is readily discovered with what plentitude of heart he gives himself to us: since he styles this sacred meat, the bread of every day, and would have us petition for it daily. Yet great attention must be paid to that purity of heart, and to those virtues which should be practiced by those who thus receive it."

St. Mary Magdalen of Pazzi, to gratify her longing desire of frequent communion, entered the Convent of St. Mary of Angels, under the Carmelitic rule, because they there communicated daily. This holy woman, frequently felt great sorrow and grief, arising from the little respect which, in general, was paid to holy communion, and from the want of a desire among Christians, of receiving it often. "I undoubtedly hold," she was used to say, "that one communion performed with heart and sentiment, is alone sufficient greatly to perfect a soul; let us pray to our Lord, that he would vouchsafe to grant us his light, which may awaken our tepidity and remissness in his holy service, especially our tardiness in receiving this bread of life, which is a fire of love." Communion was, I may say, her predominant holy passion, and in sickness, as in health, she received it daily. It happened, that some means were taken to withdraw her from this custom: "Should it be, she said, on account of my worthiness, and by the command of my Director, I will readily obey: but no other motive shall induce me to abstain from this holy sacrament, were it even to cost me my life: for without this heavenly bread, I by no means could endure the sufferings which I experience, both in body and in mind: but when I am refreshed with this food, I feel myself equal to the weight of my cross."

We read that St. Gertrude, who also communicated daily, offered up her morning actions by way of preparation for communion, and those of the afternoon in thanksgiving for so great a favor. She constantly recommended frequent communion, and was privileged by heaven, in a manner uncommon, even to other saints. For our Lord assured her, that she should never give an improper advice concerning this sacrament, and that he would so support, with his holy grace, such as she should counsel to communion, that none of them should receive unworthily. To confirm the point in question, I might copy the fourth book of the following of Christ. Grenade, Taulerus, Blosius, Rodriguez, Dupont, and an hundred other masters of spiritual matters, who unanimously teach frequent communion: for such is the doctrine of all who have served God in spirit and in truth. We shall now discuss what purity is demanded for frequent and worthy onmmunion.

CHAPTER X.

OF THE HOLINESS REQUISITE AND COMMANDED FOR WORTHY AND FREQUENT COMMUNION.

It should seem sufficiently proved, that it is evidently comformable to the views of Jesus Christ, and of his Church, that the faithful should frequently partake of this life-giving food: the man who persists in the opposite opinion, either betrays great ignorance, or wilfully shuts his eyes to obvious and palpable truths. In fact, the opponents to frequent communion, do not directly condemn it. They even seemingly approve of it on the one hand, whilst on the other, they equivalently oppose it, by too rigidly exacting, for a worthy participation of it, an uncommon fund of virtue, and of sanctity. I trust, however, that on a rational and impartial discussion of the point in hand, the most plausible arguments of such rigorists, will, of themselves, fall to the ground. For who, with any propriety, can possibly suppose, that our Redeemer would so impose upon mankind. as to invite them to frequent communion, and expect from them, at the same time, such dispositions as were beyond their reach, and superior to their strength. An assertion like this, is irrational and impious. That parent would be not only devoid of feeling, but also would be a monster, who should place food for his children where they could not reach it. Now, as our loving and merciful Lord and Father would become the daily bread to Christians, it is evident that the disposition he exacts of them for this, is such only as bears a proportion to human frailty and weakness. This is a principle not to be contested, and I think sufficient to remove every prejudice to the contrary.

For, to trace the necessary preparation for communion, from the elements of our religion, let us examine our catechetical instructions on unworthy communion, and we shall find no other document than, that we receive not sacrilegiously unless we receive in the state of mortal sin. He therefore, who is free from mortal sin, either by the innocence of his conduct, or through a sincere sorrow joined to absolution, may be assured that he does not communicate unworthily: or, in other words, he who communicates in the state of grace, communicates worthily.

To throw a better light on this subject, it is proper to distinguish two sorts of sancity; the sancity of strict precept, and that of decency and of counsel. That of strict precept, is at all times absolutely necessary for communion, and the want of it, would be productive of a sacrilege. It essentially consists in an actual exemption from mortal sin, and in being in the state of grace, through a faith which is animated by charity. The sanctity of counsel is an actual exemption from all venial sin, and an actual disposition of fervor and devotion, proportioned to the graces received. He who is free from mortal sin, is in God's holy grace and friendship, and he who possesses His friendship, is in possession of the disposition which is requisite and commanded for communion: and with this disposition, no communion can be sacrilegious. This is a certain and a Catholic truth, which to oppose or impugn, would be a deviation from faith.

Whenever our Redeemer speaks of the Eucharist, he constantly supposes, that the Christian who receives it, is in the state of grace, a state which presents him alive to view. "My flesh is truly food." Food appertains not to the dead, but to the living only: being useless to those, it is necessary to these, that being in life, they may continue to live. For which reason our Redeemer adds: "I am the bread of life, the living bread come down from heaven; this bread will preserve the life of those who shall eat of it; they shall not die." The question is here of spiritual death: and because this sacrament always presupposes spiritual life in him who receives it, it is termed by divines a sacrament of the living, that is, of those who disengaged from mortal sin live in grace.

The parable of the feast which our Redeemer delivered as a type or representation of communion, throws a light on this doctrine. The nuptial robe of which one of the guests was devoid, is sanctifying grace, without the possession of which, no one must presume to go to this banquet, under pain of being cast into outward darkness*: but lesser faults, human weakness and imperfections, though it be most adviseable to remove them as much as possible, do not exclude us from our right to the eucharistic table. A similar parable related

---

*Matth. xxii.

by St. Luke†, clearly proves that the poor and the needy, the weak and the infirm, as they are lawfully invited and convened, so they may lawfully partake of the feast. Though they labor under many disadvantages, they are alive and in God's friendship, food therefore may, and most probably will avail them.

This assertion is by no means invalidated by an expression of our Savior, where he says, "He that is clean, has only need to have his feet washed," as if it should import, that anterior to communion, even the smallest obstacles must be removed. For though it be certain that the more pure and spotless we are, the more welcome and acceptable we shall be, no other inference can be drawn from our Redeemer's words, than that great purity is counselled, but not positively commanded. In compliance therefore to this counsel, the universal custom is to recite aloud the confiteor before communion, after which, the priest gives his blessing, with a kind of absolution from lesser faults, like a whipping off the dust which gathers about the feet. It is moreover the constant practice among the faithful, to avail themselves of the

---

† Luke xiv.

sacrament of penance, even for the remission of the smallest faults, though venial sins are not a necessary, but barely a sufficient matter of that sacrament. A golden cup, whose lustre should be lessened by some particles of dust, is not less bright; so the lesser faults of a soul who is in God's friendship, destroy not the gold of charity and of grace: and nothing more is commanded for a worthy communion, than the possession of so valuable a treasure.

There are some who will say, the following words are most striking and alarming*. "Whosoever shall eat this bread, or drink the chalice of the Lord unworthily, shall be guilty of the body and blood of the Lord." And therefore we ought to stand greatly in awe, especially of frequent communion, for fear of a sacrilege. The fallacy however of this argument, is very obvious. There is no doubt but that an unworthy communion is a sacrilegious trampling under foot, the body and blood of Jesus Christ, but when and how is this crime perpetrated? What essentially constitutes and determines an unworthy communion? Nothing but a communion received in the state of

---

* 1 Cor. xi.

mortal sin. Wherefore the apostle commands self-trial and self-inspection, and if on examination, a man finds himself free from all deadly contagion, he orders him confidently to receive*, "Let him prove himself and so eat," but should there be guilt, let repentance follow, and then communion. "Let him prove himself, and so eat:" and in this supposition, no communion can be unworthy or sacrilegious. The apostle does not say let him try himself for some time, and then eat, nor yet does he say, let him prove himself, and through respect, abstain from this bread, but let him first prepare himself, and so let him eat. Whosoever therefore repents of mortal sin, which on examination he discovers; or is not guilty of any, ought to communicate frequently, and even daily, according to the advice of the said apostle.

This has been the unanimous language of the fathers: they have ever maintained that an exemption from mortal sin was indeed an indispensable condition, but at the same time a sufficient disposition for frequent communion.

Let us hear S. Cyprian on this head*: "We pray that this bread may be given to us DAILY,

---

* Cyprian in orat. Dom. Serm. 6.

lest we, who now live in Christ, and who DAILY receive the Eucharist as food of salvation, should be obliged to abstain from this heavenly bread, from the commission of some more grievous sin, and thus be separated from the body of Christ." In the opinion then of this saint, mortal sin only, is an impediment to daily communion, which if we are free from, we may communicate daily.

S. Chrysostom perfectly agrees with the former. "*To think that a long interval of time between one communion and another, is a better preparation for that duty, than purity of heart, is a mistake productive of universal disorder and confusion: he always receives opportunely, whose conscience is pure; to a Christian, all times should be like the festival of Easter." And elsewhere, we read†: "He who is not conscious of the guilt of any great sin, should communicate DAILY."

S. Hilarion in the west, joins in sentiment the the fathers of Africa and of the east‡. "If the sins you commit, are not mortal, you are not to lay aside your daily medecine of the body and blood of our Lord."

---

* Chrys. Hom 6. in c. 2. Ep. 1· ad Timoth.
† In orat. de beat. Philogon.
‡ Hil. dist. 2. de consecr.

S. Ambrose, still more emphatically affirms that‡, "He who is undeserving of DAILY communion, is equally undeserving of receiving but YEARLY, because the disposition required for one communion in the year, which is an exemption from mortal sin, is the disposition for DAILY communion. If this be your daily bread, why do you receive but once in the course of a twelve-month. RECEIVE IT DAILY."

S. Jerome, in more than one place, declares*, "That while we are not contaminated by any deadly sin, the Eucharist should be our DAILY nourishment." S. Augustine writes in similar terms†: "Carry with you to the altar, a clean heart, and should your sins be only daily failings and not mortal, reflect on what you say before you receive, *forgive us our trespasses;* if you forgive, they will be forgiven you; go therefore to the sacred table with confidence, you will receive a heavenly bread, and not poison."

The same saint claims our particular attention in the following lines: "§We are not allowed to deprive any one of communion, unless one should

---

‡ Ambr. c. in orat. dom. ex lib. 5. de Sacram. * Hier. ad Licinium. † August. in Joan. tract. 26. § August. in lib. de medicina pænitentiæ, c. 6. in medio T. 9.

spontaneously declare himself guilty of some great crime, or juridically stand convicted of any capital offense in any civil or ecclesiastical court."

To the authority of the holy fathers, I add that of our most distinguished doctors of theology, who all with one voice, assert with S. Thomas‡, "That mortal sin in a Christian, is the only positive obstacle to communion: and as every Christian has received, through baptism, a right to sit at the sacred table, it is in no one's power to deprive him of it: should he even be a public sinner, once he has done penance, he resumes his right."

The decisions also of the church, spoken by the council of Trent, are exactly of the same tenor†. "Doubtless, the more the holiness and godliness of this sacrament is made known to the Christian man, the greater should his care and attention be to receive it with great reverence and suitable purity, especially as we read in the apostle these formidable words, *he who eats and drinks unworthily, eats and drinks his own condemnation.* Let him therefore, who would communicate, attend to the command given by the said apostle, *let a man prove himself:* now the invariable custom and

---

‡ D. Tho. S. 3. p. q. 80. a. 7. & 9. † Concil. Trid. S. 13. c. 7;

practice of the church, declares that this necessary probation consists in this, that no Christian who is conscious of any mortal sin, how contrite soever he may judge himself to be, is to receive the blessed Eucharist, without having previously cleared his conscience through the sacrament of penance. This is an inviolable rule from which, the holy council declares, no one of the faithful is ever to deviate, no more than any of those, whose profession and department it is, to celebrate the holy mysteries."

From the above quotation, I reason thus: First, I coincide with the holy council, that the holiness and divinity of the Eucharist, requires great purity in communicants. Secondly, I say with the apostle, that we must prove and examine ourselves, and, with the council, that this probation essentially consists in a sacramental absolution from every grievous offense. Thirdly, I say, that to those who are unfortunately in the state of mortal sin; this probation is necessary, even among those who, from their office, are habitually in the occasion of celebrating the divine mysteries. The council however requires, in rigor, no other probation or disposition, because no other is absolutely wanting. An exemption from mortal sin, therefore, or the state of grace, is the only necessary disposition, it is consequently a disposition truly sufficient for worthy communions.

Thus, should you want to make a purchase, valued at five hundred pounds, by giving that sum, you shall be in possession; if you have this sum you doubtless have a sufficiency for the purpose, and who would say, that you must have more? The congregated fathers of the council of Trent, require no other disposition for communion, than an exempion from mortal sin: the holiness therefore which Jesus Christ, his apostles, and his Church demand for this end, is no other than the possession of God's friendship. The Oracle has spoken, who dare contradict it?

There are some however, who, through a zeal which by no means is supported by proper information and knowledge, have advanced, that the purity commanded for communion, is greater than an exemption from mortal sin. But their assertions are totally destitute of proof and argument, and clearly show, that there is an ignorant jumble made of what is of counsel, and what is of precept, contrary to the meaning of the Church, who has

---

* Bulla Alex. vii. Anno 1690.

condemned the following assertion: *Whosoever has a pure love, and is not free from all faults, must be withheld from communion.* If this perfect love were absolutely necessary for communion, communion itself would be impracticable.

Let us then steadfastly hold here, and finish this point, by giving a short, yet clear account of this Catholic doctrine. An exemption from every mortal sin, is that sanctity which makes us worthy of communion. Everything beyond, is of counsel only, not absolutely commanded; thus qualified, I shall not profane the sacrament, I shall not receive my death, condemnation and judgment; my communion will not be unworthy or sacrilegious. Should I be so fortunate as generally to be free from mortal sin, by the dwelling of the Holy Ghost within me, I may communicate often, yet not unworthily; and, if still more fortunately, I should always be free from mortal sin, I may constantly communicate, in the comfortable thought, that the disposition I am in, is such as is required and commanded by the Church.

It is therefore greatly to mistake the meaning of the Church, rashly and cruelly to withdraw from frequent commnnion, those souls whose lives are innocent, who carefully shun deadly offenses, and whose earnest labor it is, to master their rising passions.

There is a color of an argument against the above doctrine, which prevails not a little among some, of justly suspected principles, and which would insinuate, that the ancient public penances, which subsisted in various degrees, were intended for preparatives for communion: but the man who candidly is in search of truth, will clearly find in Church history, that the ancient fathers constituted those different degrees of penance, as dispositions for sacramental absolution, and not for communion. This sort of discipline has since been changed by the Church ever infallible, because ever guided by the spirit of God: the alteration is merely accidental, the essentials of this sacrament, contrition, confession and satisfaction, invariably have been the same; the whole difference is, that satisfaction formerly, was sometimes public; and now through wise and weighty reasons, it generally is private.

CHAPTER XI.

THE EXCELLENCY OF THE HOLINESS WHICH IS OF PRECEPT.

By the holiness which is of precept I understand, that degree of holiness, which is exacted from every communicant, by the law of God and his Church; now this consists essentially, as has been observed in the foregoing chapter, in an exemption from all mortal sin. It is a specious, though an absurd, as well as a dangerous and pernicious principle, to point at the infinite greatness and grandeur of God, and his incomprehensible majesty and boundless perfection, as a rule of proportion, by which we are to measure the holiness of our disposition for the blessed Eucharist. If the transcendant sancity of God is to enter into a balance, with that purity which we are to possess, if the effulgency of his majesty and grandeur is attentively to be viewed, as exacting a suitable return of worth and excellency; the purity of the angelic Host, the fervency of seraphic Love would fall infinitely short of what would be requisite. A state of perfection suitable to God's greatness, either in equality or in excellence, is absolutely impossible to man: nothing therefore can be more absurd, than to suppose, on the one hand, that such a state is exacted of us, and, on the other, that we are ever to communicate. Nothing also can be more pernicious, than a principle of this nature, the tendency of which inevitably must be to destroy the belief of a sacrament, whose institution would be totally useless, if the due disposition to receive it were absolutely unattainable.

Whereas the state of grace, or an exemption from mortal sin, is, with God's assistance, within every one's reach; and it is much to be feared, that some mistaken rigorists, pay not sufficient attention to the excellency of this desirable situation. For, though it may be termed the first or lowest degree of sanctity, it ceases not to be a most noble and heroical state, a master-piece of grace, and of a christian soul. It raises man to the friendship of his God, the only object of his happiness, and brings him to a sincere detestation of every past, as well as of all future offences: he who possesses this treasure, is stern and inflexible enough to prefer it to every other possession: parents, relations and friends, injuries and calamities, hardships, dangers, and death itself are not weighty enough in the balance: he postpones them all to this one darling object, and thus yields a sovereign preference to his Maker in competition with any of his works. This is attainable by man, this is the case of every one who is in the state of grace, which state however does not, at all times, exclude every imperfection. This preference, is truly and properly a supreme, heroic and a divine homage, and is at once admirably well shaped to the grandeur of the Almighty, and the weakness of man, and consequently is a preference so generous and so extensive as to be a sufficient, as well as a pleasing disposition for communion. I therefore repeat, that those who are happily in this disposition are properly such Christians whom Jesus Christ invites to it, and would have partake of it: of this number are all those who live piously and holily in the observance of God's laws: all, of both sexes, who lead a regular and edifying life: the crowd of the indigent and poor who are satisfied with the appointments of Providence; the opposite set of the wealthy who are liberal to their fellow creatures, and retain the fear of God: and particularly the crowd of religious people, who discharge the duties of their respective callings. My motive for being so diffuse on this head, arises from an earnest desire of removing from the minds of several, those prejudices and groundless fears which retard and obstruct many faithful and advantageous communions, from a pretence that where there intervenes any fault or failing, there ensues an unworthy communion. God avert that I ever should run down, or explode that holiness which is of counsel: or, in other words, far be it from me ever to take anything from the true value of that state which is free from every venial sin, and exempt from all attachment to it. It is much to be wished that we were all so fortunate and happy, and I most pressingly exhort all to use every endeavor to attain it. However as a righteous man, according to the language of the Holy Ghost, falls often in the day, we hardly can expect to be perfectly unspotted, though it behooves us daily to aim at greater purity of conscience; to which end, I positively assert, that frequent communion is the means most efficaciously, as well as the most expeditiously conducive. I here advance no more than the opinion of the Council of Trent, of the Fathers, and of all the ascetics. The Council tells us that the blessed Eucharist is an antidote which frees us from venial sins, from our frailties and imperfections: it consequently supposes that we are to communicate notwithstanding these imperfections: for, if we were free from them before communion, how can it be understood that communion has freed us? *Salvator noster sumi voluit sacramentum hoc, tamquam antidotum quo liberemur a culpis quotidianis.**

St. Ambrose holds the same language:† "If the blood of Jesus Christ, as often as it is consecrated, be shed for the remission of sins, I ought always to take the remedy against sin." St. Augustine, terms the blessed Eucharist a daily medicine for our weakness.

St. Francis of Sales, who stands as a perfect model to every prelate, both for the holiness of his life, and for the experiences in the due management of souls in the road to perfection, often repeats: ‡"Make it known to the worldlings that the perfect, ought frequently to communicate, because they are properly prepared for it: and the imperfect also, that they may become more perfect; the strong, lest they should become weak; and the weak, that they may become strong: the sick that they may recover health."

---

* Council Trid. Sess. 13, c. 2.   † Ambrose. l. 4. c. 6. de Sacram.
‡ Devout Life, p. 2. c. 21.

Thus it is, that those venial and daily sins, which, according to St. Augustine, a fervent recital of the Lord's Prayer is sufficient to efface, have, in daily communion, their daily remedy, through ardency of love, which this heavenly gift excites and kindles in our hearts; our daily infirmities therefore should be so far from becoming an obstacle to our daily communion, that they are precisely the motive which should induce and determine us to it. Little is the attention we pay either the medicine or to the physician, whilst we refuse to avail ourselves of it, and when it was chiefly intended for those very circumstances, on the account of which we abstain from it.

From what I here say, I beg I may not be thought to approve of any communion, which should be performed carelessly, inattentively, or out of any sinister or improper motive, nothing of the kind is ever to be countenanced or approved of. But my meaning is, that to labor under some venial sins and imperfections, into which we may frequently relapse, and which we rather suffer than we encourage, is no sort of hindrance to communion, because it is the remedy, and the best of remedies to all such complaints: *It is an antidote by which we are freed from our daily faults.*

Some here may allege the practice of some saints, who, on account of their lesser sins, abstained themselves, and caused others to abstain from holy communion. I cannot positively deny the assertion: it now and then has been the case, yet not often, and never through any precept, or from any kind of obligation, which compelled them to it: the want of the proper distinction which is to be made between what is obligatory, and what is not so, but, only of choice, will never fail to breed confusion in every debate. *Our present point in question is, whether our lesser faults oblige us to refrain from communion: and I positively affirm, they do not. The examples hinted at, bring on no precept, they possibly may be laudable, but they establish no rule. Several saints have lived in continual fasting; are we therefore under an obligation of similar austerity? There are saints who preserved their virginity in the matrimonial state; must all married people follow their example? It is the part of a preacher, of a director, and of a writer, to speak and write theologically and with precision: whereas innovators, rigorists, and weak minds, mix and jumble together practices of bare counsel with those of strict precept.

It may furthur be urged, that if the primitive

Christians communicated daily, they did so because they were living saints, and had attained to the practice of the sublime virtues: they divested themselves of what they possessed, they lived in constant prayer; like angels upon earth, they breathed forth nothing but love for Christ, and for his cross.

Plausible, but false reasoning! Had our forefathers communicated from a motive of their superior virtue, their motive would have been vanity and presumption: many of them, indeed, were holy people, but many more were very faulty and imperfect: the apostle of the Gentiles reproaches them with several of their frailties, such as their little jealousies and envies, their resentments and vanities: and St. John who communicated daily, declares, that, *If any one amongst us says, that he is free from sin, he deceives himself*, and that *the truth of God is not in him*. But did the apostle, upon this account, forbid communion? By no means: on the contrary he adds, that acknowledging our sins, we are to remember that Jesus Christ is our mediator, to whose throne we are to make application for mercy and grace. Let us take his advice, and drop all thoughts of abstaining from communion, because we are spiritually weak and infirm.

However from an expression of S. Francis of Sales, in which he dissuades daily, and even weekly communion, whilst there is left in the soul an affection to venial sin, there are some who thus do abstain to their great spiritual detriment. The affection or attachment of which the saint speaks, is a fixed and deliberate disposition to continue in the commission of lesser faults, without any endeavor, or resolution, on our part, either to avoid them, or diminish their number: in this sense, he is to be understood, and in no other. But it is hardly to be supposed, or even to be conceived, that a Christian, who communicates like a Christian, will use no kind of endeavor to purify his conscience, before he presents himself to the Lord's table. In this view, everyone has a fixed time for prayer before communion, a general pardon is asked for, a kind of general absolution is pronounced, and the sacrament of penance is mostly made use of, previously to this important action. No doubt there are some rare and particular cases, in which a director may wisely and prudently, even for venial sins only, suspend communion for a short space of time: but as these cases are very uncommon, they do not interfere with the general rule, which admits to communion those who are in lesser sins, unless we contend, that a director is vested with the power of excommunication for the commission of venial sin. Our religion however teaches us, that a venial transgression, is not a necessary, but only a sufficient matter of the sacrament of penance.

Nor should frequent relapses into the same faults and imperfections, preclude an access to the holy table. The best of us are naturally prone to evil, which when we oppose and reject, when the representation of it causes in us displeasure, the inclination we feel towards it, is not an affection for it, but barely the effect of our naturally weak and infirm texture: we really could wish to be less hasty and impatient in the occurrences of life, yet we frequently fall into faults of unreasonableness of temper: we as often condemn ourselves for our want of virtue, and feel sorrow and compunction for our deficiency.

The Eucharist often received, moderates our natural impetuosity, and corrects the faults it is productive of: a privation of this heavenly assistance, would give additional strength to our evil inclinations, and leave us destitute of means to correct them. There have been saints who perfectly moderated their humor, and overcame every passion, with the help of daily communion. S. Ignatius and S. Francis of Sales, were remarkable instances: yet they acknowledged themselves guilty of many faults and imperfections.

The truth is, that no man, though ever so perfect, can live absolutely blameless, and entirely devoid of harm: this singular privilege was solely conferred on the Mother of God; to put off therefore communion, till we had attained a purity like this, would be a most presumptuous illusion. No length of time could bring our design to bear, and the most virtuous would be unfit and unable to discharge their Easter duty; the Church has never pointed out absence from communion as a means to eradicate sin: but on the contrary, she invites and exhorts us frequently to receive it, because it is an antidote to our daily failings, and to add greater weight to her exhortations, she assures us, that such was the end for which our Redeemer originally instituted this excellent sacrament.*

Nothing therefore can be more evident, than that the reverence and respect which withholds us from communion, is an eroneous* respect, and greatly deviating from the intention of our Savior.

---

* Concil. Trid. Sess. 13.

To whom are we to give ear and credit on this subject, to the Church of God, or to her enemies? For I venture to advance, that an extravagant rigorist is a greater enemy to the Church than a loose divine, though they are both to be combatted and condemned.

I conclude this chapter with the following anecdote, which we read in the life of S. Francis of Sales. A young priest, an acquaintance of the saint, had limited his celebration of mass to Sundays and holidays. The saint, who esteemed him much, made use of the following expedient to induce him to celebrate daily. He presented him with a box which was covered with red satin, richly embroidered, and elegantly mounted, saying, "I am going to ask you a favor, which I hope you will not refuse me, for the glory of God takes part in it, and I think I know your zeal for the honor of so great a master. Command me, replied the priest. No, said the saint, I give no command, but barely demand for the present: but I make it in the name and for the love of God. While the other stood silent and astonished, the holy prelate opened the box, which was full of hosts for consecration, and continued, you are a priest, and to this sublime ministry the Lord has peculiarly called you. Would it be in character for a tradesman, a magistrate, or a physician, to confine the practice of their profession to one day in the week? You have the power of celebrating daily, why do you not make use of it? It is what you may safely do, your disposition leads you to it. Accept of this gift, and be mindful of me at the altar. The priest humbly represented his real unworthiness, his youth, his want of mortification and recollection, and expressed his fears of abusing so great a mystery. For my part, the saint replied, I am of opinion, (and I think I am guided by the spirit of God) that the very reasons which you allege to the contrary, are most cogent motives for an immediate acquiescence to my request: the holy Eucharist received, will strengthen and ripen your youth, will weaken and lessen your temptations, will consolidate you in virtue, and better than any other means, will fit you for a proper discharge of your functions." The ecclesiastic yielded, and followed the advice the remainder of his life.

CHAPTER XII.

THE APOSTLES AND THE CHURCH OF GOD HAVE AT ALL TIMES ADMITTED TO COMMUNION, THOSE WHO POSSESSED THIS HOLINESS OF PRECEPT.

Too many are the books dispersed through the Christian world, which, by constantly insinuating the great respect which is due to the eucharistic sacrament, would fain persuade their readers that the preparation exacted for communion, cannot be too great, and that penance for past sins cannot be protracted to too great a length, before we should venture to partake of this holy mystery: they therefore would have us believe, that a sinner, who, in good earnest, has returned to his duty, is still to be put to trials of a lasting duration, previously to his admission to the sacrament: so great is the reverence, so profound the veneration which is transcendently due to it!

It is however beyond a doubt, notwithstanding these plausible colorings of awe and respect, that every sinner, who is duly absolved from his sins, is in the state of grace, and by that alone, is sufficiently qualified for communion. Of this certain truth, we have irrefragable proofs from the days of the apostles, down to the present age.

The eight thousand Jews and Gentiles who received the light of faith from two of S. Peter's sermons, were undoubtedly suddenly converted, and as suddenly baptised. They were also great sinners, for the apostle reproaches them with the death of our Lord, *auctorem vitæ interfecistis:* immediately however after baptism, they were admitted to daily communion. The Christians therefore in our days, who are penitent and have been absolved, how great soever their sins may have been, as they receive the same sanctifying grace, the same holy spirit, which qualified the primitive proselytes for frequent communion, are equally entitled to the same advantages; unless there should be a better school for religious documents than that of the apostles. The position which imports that absolution and communion should be withheld from great sinners for a long space of time, is censured and proscribed by the church, and is virtually or equivalently condemned by our blessed Redeemer, in the parable of the prodigal, whose father immediately, on his return, receives him into favor: and the moment he forgives, he admits him to the feast. A striking image is here presented of the sacraments of penance and of the Eucharist.

The incestuous Corinthian whom S. Paul had excommunicated*, was by the same apostle, speedily restored to the participation of holy things, on account of the intense sorrow which he expressed for his sin: the rest of his brethren were desired to pay him every charitable attention, and afford him every comfort in his distress. Who will say that S. Paul was not actuated by the spirit of his master?

We read also that the loving and beloved S. John, having brought a young man to the knowledge of Jesus Christ, placed him, for a while, under the care of an Asiatic bishop, the better to preserve him in the fear of God. The youth however fell from his first fervor, and gradually became so profligate, as to head a band of robbers, who, taking possession of a mountain, difficult of access, infested the neighborhood with plunder and rapine. Meanwhile, the apostle happened to meet with the bishop to whose care he had consigned the unhappy man: the prelate replied that

---

* Cor. ii.

he was dead: dead! said the other, of what sort of death? he is dead to God. At which the apostle rent his garment, sighed and groaned, saying, "I cannot doubt but I left in you a faithful guardian of the soul of your brother: let me have a horse directly, and a guide to show me the way." The holy man with all speed made to the mountain, but being interrupted by the sentinel, he desired to be brought before his captain, and his request was complied with. The captain sternly waited for his approach with sword in hand, but on discovering who his visitor was, shame and confusion took the place of his fierceness, and set him to flight. The saint followed him, and in paternal accents said, "My son, why do you fly? Why do you fly from your father, from a harmless defenceless old man? My son, take pity on me; fear not, you may still hope for salvation: I will be your ransom with Jesus Christ, I will pawn my soul for yours, believe me and stop." At these words he yielded and stopped: trembling, sorrowful and bathed in tears, he threw himself at the feet of his friendly pursuer, who received him with open arms, and mingled his tears of joy, with those which compunction had forced from his repenting child. He animated and consoled him with all paternal solicitude; and Eusebius* assures us that he did not leave him till he had restored him to the church, and to a participation of the sacrament.

Tertullian informs us†, that the Roman church admitted to the sacraments, at two different times, the heresiarchs, Marcion, and Valentin, on the acknowledgement of their errors, and Marcion had a promise of pardon for a third relapse, but a sudden death deprived him of the full fruition of it.

S. Irænous relates that Cerdon another heresiarch, had been often, on his repeated resilience, made partaker of the communion of the church. Nor was he ever condemned to trials of long duration, or to any public penance. This mode of atonement, was not at that period in use: at no time indeed was it ever more than an accidental ceremony, which was as wisely introduced at one period, as it was prudently dropped at another. The true spirit of penance, though it has occasionally assumed various forms, has, in all ages, invariably been the same. Every repenting sinner was always bound to detest and confess his sins, as well as to satisfy and atone for them: nor is this atonement so very easy and practicable as

---

* Euseb. l. 2. Hist. Eccles. c. xvii. † Tertul. l. de præscript. c. xxx.

some may imagine. We do not very readily manifest our many weaknesses and miseries, especially when self-accusation puts us to shame: a sovereign aversion to sin, a serious reparation of past scandal, a complete restitution of unlawful property, a reparation of injured virtue and fame, a perfect reconciliation with all the world, and a total forgiveness of every injury, make up the compound character and spirit of penance, which, upon reflection, will not readily be allowed to be of an easy acquisition. It is however an acquisition absolutely necessary, whilst at the same time it is intirely sufficient for communion. The Fathers exacted no more, and several of them zealously reprimanded such Bishops and Pastors, as imprudently withheld their flock from absolution and the Eucharist.

S. Leo writes to Bishop Theodore: "We must not be diffident in the distribution of the gifts of God, neither are we to overlook the sighs and tears of self-accusing sinners, especially when we may hope that the desire they have formed of being reconciled to their Maker, proceeds from his merciful inspiration."

The same Saint is still more emphatic, in his letter to the Bishops of Vienna: "Communion is not easily to be refused to a Christian. . . A soul in whose behalf the blood of Jesus Christ has been shed, is not to be afflicted with so severe a chastisement, which would render her defenceless before her enemies, and expose her too openly to the fury of their darts."

S. Prosper coincides in opinion with the former*, and by a fresh reason with which he supports it, shows how justly he linked discretion with zeal: "If the weak and infirm are deprived of communion, because they are somewhat indocile and intractable, they either will sink under the weight of an excessive grief, which will render vain the efforts of their pastors to bring them back to their duty; or they will give themselves up to a licentious way of life, which will render their salvation desperate."

The great S. Chrysostom says: "Let no one tell me, my conscience is loaded with sins: the space of these five days, is sufficient to repent in, provided that you are sober, watchful and attentive to diminish the number of them, and to amend your faults: be in no pain concerning the shortness of time, only reflect that the Lord is merciful.

---

* Prosp. l. 2. de contemptu.

The Ninivites in the course of three days, averted from their heads the vengeance of heaven.*" And elsewhere he says: "One day alone is enough to purify and sanctify our souls; nay, we may amend and get well, in less than an hour†."

St. Augustine entertains the same sentiments of mercy: "Although our repentance be but of short standing, if we have entered upon it with bitterness of heart, we must firmly hope for forgiveness: for our Lord attends more to the sincerity of our heart, than to the space of time."

But a mistaken reverence for communion, will still insinuate, that it seems more decent, and more becoming a penitent sinner to abstain from this awful mystery, till he gains strength and acquires a competent degree of virtue and holiness, which would render him more worthy, and his communion more fruitful.

This however, like every other motive for retardment, is void of solidity and reason. I might as well advance that a man, who is on his recovery from a fit of sickness, had better wait for a perfect recovery, before he begins to take proper nourishment. A sincere penitent, although peni-

---

* Chrys. Hom. de. S. Pigon. T. i.   † Hom. de Perdit. Judæ. T. 5.

tent, is doubtless weak and feeble: and this heavenly food is designedly intended for him, that he may recover his strength. Whilst he is debarred from it, he will ever languish. *I am the bread of life, that he who eats of it, may not die.* The Eucharist therefore, is, as the Council of Trent expresses it, the health and strength of our souls, and the primary design of its institution was at once to nourish us, and shield us from sin. If we abstain from it, we shall be languid and unguarded from evil: if we receive it often, we bid defiance to our worst enemies.

"It will be more or less with you, if you communicate often, says St. Francis of Sales, as it was with Mithridates, who through fear of being poisoned, used himself daily to a certain quantity of poison, which so much invigorated him, that when he would be poisoned, he could not effect it.

"If mankind, continues this saint,[*] might have preserved their bodily lives, by means of the tree of life, which God had placed in the terrestrial Paradise; why may not christians preserve their spiritual lives, by means of this bread of life? A little honey or sugar conserves most delicate and

---

[*] Devout Life, c. 20.

perishable fruit, such as cherries, strawberries and apricots. Where then is the wonder, if our souls, how weak soever they may be of themselves, should be preserved from the corruption of sin, when once they have been penetrated with the virtue and sweetness of the incorruptible blood of Jesus Christ." There are then no means so powerful and efficacious to preserve a penitent sinner in grace and in virtue, as frequent communion. It was through this help, that the above mentioned saint, converted a multitude of sinners into eminent saints. In so doing he followed the example of the apostles, and of all apostolic men in every Christian age. St. Vincent Ferrer, St. Philip of Neri, St. Cajetan, St. Vincent of Paul, St. Francis Xavier, employed this sacrament with the greatest success, for the reformation and sanctification of their neighbors.

Notwithstanding these many striking proofs, which assert the propriety of frequent communion, it still has its opponents, who by various arguments, as well as through various motives, endeavor to withdraw mankind from the chief source of their happiness. It would seem, they will say, reasonable, that a great sinner should proportion the severity of his penances, to the magnitude of his former guilt, it consequently would seem reasonable, that as communion is the greatest of favors, to refrain from it would be the greatest of punishments.

The fallacy of this argument is laid open by St. Ambrose: "Those who abstain from the divine sacrament from a spirit of penance, are severer on themselves than they should be, for while they inflict on themselves this punishment, they deprive themselves of a most efficacious remedy."

Besides are we to believe that the idea of christian repentance and atonement for sin, is confined to a life of solitude, to fasting, hair shirts, and other bodily macerations? These are, indeed, helps, they are very conducive to the penitential spirit, but they are not the constituents of it: the love of God, the practice of christian virtues, the mortification of the inward man, the suppression of the irregular follies of passion, a moderation in prosperity, a resignation in adversity, a reference to God in every action, are the soul and life of this excellent virtue, to the acquisition and practice of which, no help is so conducive as frequent communion, so no virtuous deed is so great an ingredient to it, as this same holy action frequently repeated.

Some stern and severe minded people, freely stigmatize this facility of admitting sinners to the sacraments, as a laxity in morals, and a deviation from proper discipline. But what conduct is there in life, how prudent and perfect soever it may be, which is not exposed to obloquy, and liable to groundless censure and reproach? However, such meek, and tender-hearted pastors, who are thus indulgent, have every motive of comfort in the thought, that the milder they are with a penitent delinquent, the more perfect is their resemblance to their divine Master, who was meekness itself to every sinner, and disdained not familiarly to mix and converse with them. And, though the Pharisees were lavish in their calumnies against him, as overstretching and subverting the Mosaic law, he continued in the same mild and paternal tenor, and even more loudly proclaimed to the world, "That he was not come for the righteous, but for sinners: and that those who were in health, stood not in need of a physician, but such only as were sick. I am for mercy, and I reject your offerings: white-washed sepulchres outwardly, within you are base corruption; an exterior show of penance, is most to your taste, as it dazzles the eyes of men, it brings home to you their esteem.

For my part, I am for the penitence of the heart, my yoke is sweet, and my burden is light: as to you, you impose on others enormous loads, which you yourselves will not touch, not even with the tip of your fingers."

The spirit of rigorism has been at all times ostentatious in heretics: witness the Mountanists, the Novatians, Tertullian and others. The spirit of meekness has ever been the distinctive mark of all truly apostolical men, and in our latter days it was the peculiar characteristic of St. Francis of of Sales: who once being told, that some took scandal at the ease and condescension which he used with sinners, made answer, that he thought it was better to make sinners penitent, than to make them desperate. I had rather lead them gently to purgatory, than drive them rashly to hell. But it was replied, one may damn himself through too great a condescension: to which he said, with a smile, if damnation must be the consequence of an excessive indulgence, and an overflow of kindness, I would prefer the loss of heaven, occasioned by such an excess, to damnation, which should be the effect of excessive harshness and severity. S. Odilon was of the same sentiment, and expressed himself almost in the same words, as we read in the history of his life, written by Peter Damian. These great saints thought with, and held the language of St. Paul, who wished to be accursed for the sake of his brethern.

When our blessed Lord sent his apostles to convert the world, he did not say, learn from me to create new worlds, to raise the dead, or to rebuke sinners, but learn from me to be meek and humble of heart. I send you like sheep and lambs into the midst of wolves; and those approved themselves truly apostolic, who, by their meekness, changed the wolves themselves into the nature of lambs.

CHAPTER XIII.

FREQUENT COMMUNION IS THE MOST POWERFUL AND EFFICACIOUS HELP TO SALVATION.

The greatness of the end which our dear Lord proposed to himself, when he was pleased to institute this wonderful sacrament, must, doubtless, bear a proportion with the greatness of that power and bounty which are displayed as often as he admits us to his sacred table: nay, it even seems that this merciful design, of establishing a most intimate union with his creatures, is still greater and more astonishing than the mighty exertion of his power. A design like this is the fairest opening to all the treasures of heaven, and by giving us, as our nourishment, his adorable body and blood, he lifts us up to his own level, and together with himself, he makes us partake of all that he himself is in possession of; so that we become, in the language of the Royal Prophet, *like Gods*,* or as St. Peter expresses it, *you are partakers of the Divine nature*.†

The flesh of a God is truly our food, and this inestimable food imparts immortality, and a life divine. "As I live for my Father, so he that eats of my flesh, shall for me, and through me, live a life everlasting and divine, he shall dwell in me, and I in him." Actuated by an excess of an incomprehensible love, Jesus Christ under the sacramental veils, hiddenly communicates to every partaker, while on earth, his divine nature, as a pledge of that open and full communication both of himself and of his glory, which awaits us in the abodes of eternal bliss. Wonderful was his love, when, at the incarnation, he assumed the nature of man, but yet more wonderfully is this love dis-

---

* Ps. 81. † Divinæ consortes naturæ. 2. Pet. L

played, when he gives himself to all men, as a life-giving nourishment. When he first came, he only united himself to our common nature; upon leaving us, he chose to be united after a real and a most intimate manner to each of us in particular.

Holy communion therefore, is of all favors the greatest which the Creator can bestow on his creatures; it is the choicest blessing, and the best of gifts: and to those who frequently partake of it, it is the most powerful and efficacious help to salvation. The sacraments of baptism and of penance, are great marks of an unbounded love, and greatly forward our happiness; the one frees us from original, the other from actual guilt. Both also confer actual grace, but not always for any length of time sufficient, to preserve us in the love and fear of our Maker: besides those two sacraments, another was requisite, whose peculiar virtue it should be to support our weakness, and preserve us from danger, and this, through the eucharistic bread, is admirably well effected. This strengthening food confirms us in, and greatly adds to the graces which penance obtains; it revives the languid, invigorates the weak, rouses the tepid, and animates the most timid to the boldest virtue. Frequent communion therefore is transcendently, that great help, to which is annexed preference in grace, that only sacrament, which, of its own nature, has power and efficacy sufficient to preserve a soul, for any space of time, from the deadly contagion of sin.

The words of our Redeemer are an irrefragable proof*. "My flesh is truly food: it is the bread of life; he who shall eat of it, shall live for ever, and shall not die the death of sin . . . without this bread, you shall not have life in you." And the infallible criterion of the meaning of our Lord, the interpretation of the church, assures us, that the Eucharist is intended as the spiritual food of Christians, and as an antidote, which at once frees us from our daily faults, and preserves us from mortal commissions, and consequently preserves us in grace.

The other sacraments, though they confer grace, are at best but foreign vehicles of it: but in the Eucharist, Christ in person bestows grace, gives life, and wards off death: where He dwells, there is holiness itself, joined to an infinite aversion to sin. The Philistines placed the ark of the covenant in the temple of Dagon: but the impious

---

* John vi.

statue was soon found prostrate at the foot of the ark: being restored to its former state, the following day it was found disfigured and maimed. If the bare type of this great sacrament produced such wonderful effects, what virtue and efficacy may we hope for, from a frequent participation of the reality? Communion, more efficaciously than any other means, saps and destroys the empire which vice and bad habits too naturally assume over us, and has a particular tendency to subversion of self-love, the grand source of our many miseries. When we communicate often, we often enjoy the presence and power of the gracious and benevolent Jesus, who, during His mortal life, gave sight to the blind, hearing to the deaf, speech to the dumb, health to the sick, life to the dead, and inward peace to those who were tormented by devils. The hand of the Lord is not less kind now, than it was then, the same and similar blessings will continue to flow from the same source, if we approach to it with confidence. "Virtue went out from Him, and healed all*."

"If God," says the apostle†, "take our part, what enemy can molest us?" And if God fre-

---

* Luke vi. 19. † Rom. viii.

quently reign within us, what harm can befall us? He therefore is strong indeed, whom Jesus Christ shields with his presence; as on the contrary weak and unfortified must he be, who shuns His heavenly presence or seldom communicates. Invincible is the Christian in his spiritual warfare, who is thus protected, because from communion, he derives more succor, than by any other established means of salvation. By eating this food, he is strictly united to Christ, nay, transformed into his Redeemer, and therefore may say with S. Paul[*], "It is no longer I, but it is Jesus Christ who lives in me." He lives in him, makes Himself over to him, and profusely bestows on him every other blessing: in other means He sets bounds to his liberality: in the Eucharist, Christ gives Himself in person with all His treasures, unlimited in His promises, unlimited in His love, unlimited in His gifts. Moreover, as communion, upon the removal of mortal sin, was designed as an infallible application of the merits of Christ, it must, of its own nature, produce a grace which will be victorious over every inordinate affection, and will furnish the soul with most powerful helps to triumph over

---

[*] Gal. ii. 20.

her natural inconstancy, and the rudest attacks she can be exposed to. The sunny beams in an unclouded atmosphere, do not so powerfully enlighten, purify, and warm the earth, as Jesus Christ in the Eucharist enlightens, warms and transports the soul who is disingaged from mortal sin.

It is however true, that as the influence of the sun is proportioned to the cultivation of the soil, so the effect, which results from communion, is analogous to the dispositions of the communicant: where there is no mortal sin, it always confers grace. But this grace is more or less valuable and precious, as we are more or less holy and pure. The Eucharist produces this effect in common with other sacraments: but moreover, it bestows a sacramental specific grace, as the Divines express it, which is peculiar to itself, and is a grace of spiritual refection, or spiritual nourishment, according to the words of our Reneemer, *My flesh is truly food.*

He that eats of My flesh, dwells in Me, and I in him: that is, when we communicate, we receive the humanity and divinity of Jesus Christ, the former leaves us when the species are consumed; the latter continues to abide in us, and we abide in it.

The Divinity dwells in us with an additional love, which continues to nourish our mind with pious thoughts and desires, with fresh illustrations, and devout sentiments; all which, at seasonable occurrences, prompt us to virtue, and forward us to perfection.

This singular power and efficacy of frequent communion, is also the most conspicuous help which is given us to salvation, whether we consider it previously or subsequently to the reception of it: in both lights, it equally presents itself to our view, as wonderfully exciting to the holiest dispositions, and the most heroical virtues. In fact, what a diligent preparation will not the following thought be productive of, to-day, I am to receive my God? What care and attention, what sorrow and compunction must be the result of it? Even on the eve of that happy day, there is more recollection, more prayer, a closer, and a more serious communication with the God of mercy.

After communion, the presence of a God at once fills us with humility, and transports us with love: our hope and confidence, after so striking a pledge of bounty, move towards a degree of certainty of obtaining every blessing, and as our faith revives and brightens, we are animated with the tenderest sentiments of gratitude: silent are our passions on this awful occasion, while all the powers of our soul unite to adore Him in person, and freely consecrate themselves in future, to the glory of His holy name. A visit from a God! What puissant impressions must not this consideration make, even on a soul immersed in tepidity? How efficaciously must it not engage us in future, to follow the exhortation of the Apostle, that despising all worldly desires, we may lead a sober, righteous and pious life, in full hope of that great glory, of which this sacrament has given us the greatest foretaste. The oftener therefore we partake of it, the oftener shall we be in those happy dispositions, the more habituated shall we be to every virtuous sentiment, and godly desire.

Penetrated with, and well convinced of this great truth, St. Chrysostom loudly proclaimed that, "We come from this sacred table* like lions, strong and animated with the fire of Divine love, and even most formidable to the infernal host." This adorable and life-giving food, has enabled millions of martyrs to triumph over the sharpest torments, and death itself in all its most ghastly

---

* Tamquam leones flammas spirantes ex hac mensa discedimus, terribiles facti diabolo. Hom. 61. ad pop. Antioch.

shapes: it has raised thousands of tender virgins above the weakness of their sex, and brought them to the height of the most heroic virtue: instead of anguish and despair, it has given comfort and even inexpressable sweetness to thousands, who were seemingly oppressed with every species of woe, and were drinking to the dregs, the cup of every human adversity and misfortune: it has been the support and life of apostolic men, in their tedious and painful labors: it has encouraged anchorites in their fastings and austerities, and sweetened their lonesome solitudes: it has preserved from the general corruption of the world, thousands of fervent Christians, whilst it has brought others back to their duty, and established them victorious over their most inveterate habits and evil inclinations. From these, and similar pious considerations, our holy Church pours forth the following Canticle, "The faithful and the servants of God are multiplied by virtue of this heavenly wheat.*"

Such then is the Evangelical system, which our Lord has established concerning our daily bread. Our spiritual weakness is so great, that, like our

---

* Ex adipe frumenti multiplicati sunt fideles. Ex Off. SS. SS.

bodily wants, we stand in need of a particular help to preserve for a length of time, the life of our soul; this assistance is the holy Eucharist, which is also the commencement of life everlasting. But as the bare lighting up a lamp would not produce a lasting flame without a continued supply of oil; and as boiling water, if long removed from the fire, would soon return to its pristine coldness; in like manner is a Christian frequently to communicate, if he would preserve the light of grace, and keep up the fire of divine love. He who enters upon this holy practice, will soon experience the powerful influence of so great a sacrament, and the wonderful increase of his faith, of his hope and of his charity. In short, he who eats of the flesh of the son of man, shall live the life of Christ, that is, shall be like-minded with Him.

It is therefore greatly to be wished that those who are charged with the important care of souls, would imitate, in their conduct with their flock, the example of the angel who appeared to the prophet Elisha: the fugitive prophet, greatly apprehensive of the wrath of Queen Jesabel, had walked in the deserts so long and so precipitately, that, at last quite weary and spent, he laid down and slept. Mount Horeb was the place which the

Lord had ordered him to retire to for safety, but from where he then was, he had a journey to take of forty long days and nights. While thus at rest, an Angel came and waked him saying, *rise Prophet and eat*: he looks and sees a loaf of bread which had been baked in ashes, and by it a pitcher of water: he ate and drank of what was before him, and again went to sleep: the Angel spoke to him a second time and said, *rise and eat, for long yet is your journey.* He did as he was commanded, after which he began his journey, and by virtue of that refreshment, he performed it with ease and alacrity, and reached the mountain of God, Horeb. This bread was a type of the eucharistic banquet: what assistance may we not hope for from this substantial repast, on our road to the eternal mansion of bliss, while a faint emblem of it supported the Prophet, during forty days and forty nights?

Thus then should Christians be spoken to, when the question is to exhort them to communion: if you be sincerely penitent, if you shun the occasions of sin, and dread the allurements of vice, rise and eat, not of a bread which is brought you by an Angel of the Lord, but by the Lord Himself; eat of the blessed Eucharist, and eat of it often, and your repentance will be lasting, your alarms of danger will disappear; from weak, you will become strong, and from tepid, you will become fervent: this heavenly bread virtually contains every help, removes every obstacle, imparts every blessing. And you timorous souls, who readily tire in the path of virtue, you whom the length of the journey, or the obstacles which you either meet, or apprehend to meet with, so easily terrify, you who lose courage at the shadow of a cross temptation, or any sort of trial, rise and communicate often, the bread you will eat, is the bread of the strong and of the robust: it will lift you up above your former weakness, and even above yourselves, and will teach you to look down with contempt upon every obstacle to salvation. In short, I could wish to be heard by all who inhabit the Christian world, whom I earnestly exhort to communicate often: you have no means given you so efficacious as frequent communion, to facilitate the way to happiness, no means so powerful as frequent communion to secure to you the possession of happiness. This eucharistic virtue not only affects and transforms a Christian soul after a most wonderful manner, but frequently also has alone supported in perfect health, the bodies of several servants of God, for a considerable length of time. It is what we read of S. Sabas Abbot, S. Catharine of Sienna, the Abbot S. John, and of many other holy recluses, who, for months, lived on no other food, than this most adorable sacrament.

CHAPTER XIV.

FREQUENT COMMUNION IS OUR GREATEST COMFORT AND HAPPINESS IN THE WAY OF SALVATION.

I know not by what kind of spirit those people are actuated, who are for ever offering to Christian ears and eyes austere duties to be discharged, hard and severe obligations to be fulfilled, and who, seemingly unmindful of the many comforting truths, which the law of grace, above every other, most graciously affords, are busy in coloring our happy state, with truths only alarming and terrifying. We by no means are thus tutored and informed by our merciful Redeemer, who comfortingly assures us that the tender name, which by way of excellency, our God is pleased to assume over us, is that of father; and His will is, that in our prayers, our addresses should begin with that endearing appellation. Jesus Christ styles Himself our brother, our Physician, the Lamb who takes away the sins of the world, and a Shepherd so faithful and loving, as to give His life for His flock. His gospel is the reign of the God of bounty: the reign of mercy and of peace. He demands and claims our love, because He first loved us, and still continues to love us: and if we return love for love, we infallibly engage Him to secure our happiness. His yoke is sweet, and whatever burden He imposes on us, conveys peace and joy. *You shall find rest unto your souls.* Rejoice, says the apostle, and I repeat it, be extreemly glad, because the Lord is near and close at hand: and the royal prophet emphatically invites us all to serve God with alacrity and joy.

The Christian therefore must be very inattentive to the great advantages of his holy religion, who views it only in the light which terrifies him, or suffers himself to be disheartened at the apparent difficulty of salvation. Let him only reflect on the incomparable blessings which accrue from frequent communion, and he will be forced to own, that, independently of all other means, he is here furnished not only with the most powerful, but also with the most easy and most comforting help to salvation.

This pleasing truth will clearly show itself, if

we compare the advantages, which are peculiar to the Eucharist, with the difficulty which attends other gospel rules and counsels, though they are equally pointed out as means to happiness. Continual prayer and fasting, an absolute and general self-denial; a contempt of the world and of all that belongs to it; a free abnegation of will and of property which is to be made the inheritance of the poor; a perpetual recollection, and an invariable attention to the most painful and humiliating deeds of mercy: an uniform meekness and moderation, and the strictest virginal chastity; at these and such like proposals, self-love takes the alarm, and weak nature startles and recoils.

Whereas frequent communion, a repeated intimacy and union with Jesus Christ, is a smoother path, and better accomodated to our extreme weakness. Love guides us in every step, and where love is, there, neither pain nor labor is found. Taste and you will experience in frequent communion a plentitude of sweetness, which is peculiar to the Lord our God, especially when He gives Himself in the Eucharist. Here we receive correction for our failings, but the reprimand is paternal; our wounds are healed, but gentle and almost imperceptible is the hand that effects the cure: our hearts are purified, but unfelt is the violence which is used to purify us: we divest ourselves of the old, and put on a new man, but nothing intervenes forbidding in the change; we become victorious almost without combat. Communion imperceptibly withdraws, and even separates us from ourselves, and no convulsion is felt in the separation: it detaches us from every earthly object, and unites us to our Creator, and pleasing is the translation of our affections from one object to the other. Make experiment of it, communicate often: you will discover it to be a sovereign remedy against every evil, an inexhaustible source of every heavenly delight, for so does the Church proclaim it, *panem de cœlo præstitisti eis, omne delectamentum in se habentem.* Thousands have acknowledged, and thousands daily continue to experience this truth.

I go further, and add, that holy communion, on account of the facility with which it may be received, is, at times, almost the only means, which many Christians have in their power to make use of, to forward their salvation. Fervent and assiduous prayer, hardly can fall to the lot of those, whose station of life involves them in the bustle of worldly concerns; family inthralments, and unavoidable solicitudes strongly oppose the quietude of much prayer; liberalities to the poor, come within the power of a few, most are either poor themselves, or have families to provide for. Fasting, and other corporal austerities become impracticable to infirm constitutions, and to those who are obliged to labor. Idleness, the root of every evil, should be removed by a becoming occupation, and the dangerous rest and inactivity which attend on riches, should have their remedy to preserve the balance. To be sincere in the business of salvation, it seems expedient that you should quit the world, and take to retirement: but a wife and children compel you to continue in the hurry of life: the world, your affairs, and occupations, your situation in life, continually start new obstacles, and, as you advance in years, difficulties grow under your steps; what remedy, what help can you find in so great a distress? the only means left for several, the only means which bear any proportion with their weakness, and with the dangers they are exposed to, is frequent communion. The poor and the rich, the swordsman and the penman, the mechanic and merchant, the married and unmarried, the healthy and sick, all may conveniently partake of this adorable sacrament, and all may draw from it every suitable succor, without detriment to constitution, inattention to family, neglect of employment, or necessity of retiring from society: no impossibility, nor yet difficulty can reasonably be alleged in the use we should make of the Eucharist, for every one may communicate often, with every imaginable facility.

Inexcusable therefore must those Christians be, who suffer themselves to linger and die spiritually, for want of this heavenly nourishment, whilst it is the readiest and the best preservative from sin.

But, waiving for the present the other means of salvation and their respective difficulties, let us consider the advantage of frequent communion, without analogy, as it is in itself, even in this light it will evidently appear to be the sovereign happiness of man during his mortal pilgrimage.

In fact, what do we actually aspire to, and what is at present the chief object of our warmest wishes? It is, I presume, the fruition of God, and the full possession of Him in the abodes of bliss: but while our hopes are protracted, and while we continue in the pleasing expectation of that moment which, by a happy dissolution, is to crown our wishes, we cannot but acknowledge, that, for the present, our greatest happiness is to possess this God in His sacrament, in which He has wonderfully veiled the awful effulgence of His infinite Majesty, the better to enable us to approach Him in our mortal bodies, to partake of the treasure of graces, and taste the charms of His Divinity. O! incomprehensible goodness of our living God! Never was a people so blessed and exhalted as we are; we may possess, at pleasure, the delight of angels, and enjoy, at will, the rapturous bliss of heaven! What heart can extend its wishes beyond an enjoyment like this, and who would not taste daily of this torrent of pleasure, whilst there lived in his breast a spark of charity?

The ecstacies and visions which the lives of the saints furnish us ideas of, are sometimes stimulating motives to tread in their footsteps: we admire the wondrous condescension of the Most High in favor of His faithful servants, and, were it not for a conscious unworthiness on our part, we could almost wish to bear a resemblence with them. But great as these favors may seem, they fall infinitely short of the benefit of the Eucharist, in which there is not a bare vision, but a personal visit from Jesus Christ. One communion alone, eminently transcends, in price and value, all such extraordinary raptures and delights.

We may have often wished that, like Magdalen, we might bewail our sins at the feet of our Redeemer, or like Martha, that we could afford Him lodging and food, or, like the apostles, that we had been brought up at His school, or, like Joseph and Simeon, that we had carried Him in our arms, or, like Joseph and Mary, we had been spectators of His Divine conduct: ah! Christians, exclaims S. Chrysostom, why from ye these vain wishes? "In the Eucharist there is* the same Jesus Christ whom you lodge in your heart, and by frequent communion, you daily renew the same mysteries of tenderness and love. You see Him, you touch Him, you eat Him." Envy not therefore, a Magdalen, Martha, or the apostles, Joseph or Mary: fortunate is the nation of Christians! a God comes daily upon earth, to inebriate them with ineffable delights†!

Happy, ten times happy is the Christian, who frequently feasts at this heavenly banquet: his lot, in one sense, is preferable to that of the spirits above: each communion adds to his happiness, each communion, by redoubling his love, gives

---

* Vellem ipsius formam aspicere, vestimenta . . . . . ecce eum tangis vides, manducas: ipse vero tibi concedit, non tantum videre, verum et manducare et tangere et intra te sumere. Chrysost. hom. 6. † Calix meus inebrians quam præclarus est. Psal. xxii.

new lustre to his future crown of glory. He sweetly and leisurely drinks, with growing merit, of the same inebriating cup, which incessantly holds in raptures the inhabitants of the heavenly Jerusalem; and closely unites himself to the God of all comfort, while the God of all comfort, unboundedly communicates Himself to Him. Careless and unmindful of all but of his God, he sees, hears and lives but for Him. He knows no expression, he is tenderly compelled to a more amorous silence. Those fervent souls, who have often fed at this delicious repast, are no strangers to my meaning: Jesus Christ takes possession of them, reigns over them, and lives in them; He lifts up their thoughts to heaven, inspires them with a contempt of the world, rectifies their inclination, moderates their appetites, and gradually, though insensibly, transforms them into Himself.

Thus, when an earthly prince pitches on a spot of ground for a resort for relaxation and pleasure, how ungrateful soever the soil and situation may be, it presently assumes a new form, it becomes pleasant and delightful: every visit produces additional decoration, ornament and beauty. Whereas these places which are unfrequented and neglected by their masters, soon return to their pristine ungraceful state, and, in spite of their natural advantages, lose every attraction and charm.

But the most wonderful effect which flows from this heavenly banquet, is that admirable ease and facility, with which we are enabled to practice every Christian duty, though never so unpleasing and reluctant to nature. In fact, who has not experienced, that, on the day of communion, prayer, fortitude, recollection, and every restraining obligation, were devoid of irksomeness and disgust; their bitterness, on that occasion, was turned to sweetness, and their thorns into roses. The same shall we often experience, if we communicate often.

CHAPTER XV.

FREQUENT COMMUNION IS VAINLY OPPOSED BY SINNERS AS WELL AS BY SOME VIRTUOUS PEOPLE.

There have been in every Christian age, both loose and fervent Christians, who, falling into the same mistaken notion, concerning religion, and the respect which is due to the Eucharist, have acted in concert, by abstaining from it: it seems therefore important to lay open the fallacy they rest upon, and remove the dangerous masks, which so plausibly maintains the appearance of rectitude. Some of their most trite and prevailing pertexts shall now come under inspection, which, when once we have removed, the others, I trust, will be equivalently confuted.

Some, with an apparent face of sanctity, hold the following language: I do not, it is true, communicate often: but I obey the Church, and discharge my Easter duty: the weight and multiplicity of my affairs do not permit a more frequent participation of the awful mysteries; but while I comply with church discipline, I can entertain no scruples of deficiency in my obligations.

This mode of reasoning, obviously leads us to conclude, that worldly business is the chief employ of man, and that he answers best the end for which he is created, who is the most successful, or at least, the most diligent in his temporal concerns. Whereas the dictates of our religion directly contradict all such principles, and establish that salvation alone, is the only point that man should have in view; which should he overlook or neglect, the possession of the world besides, would be entirely unavailable to him. Now what great solicitude can that man have, for the welfare of his soul, who only once a year, thinks seriously of saving himself, and who only once a year makes use of these means, which are the most conducive to his salvation. That faith, must forever be erroneous, which withdraws us from, and leads us not to Christ: he who rightly believes, who hopes and loves as a Christian ought to do, is not solaced by absence from, but by union with his Maker. How slender is the friendship between two neighbors, who visit each other but once in a year? How deficient in filial duty is that son, who, though frequently asked to his Father's table, accepts of the invitation but once in a twelvemonth?

The truth is, those who limit their communion to Easter, are not led to any such restriction, by any religious principle: they are actuated by pride and self-love; by a fear of the censure of the world, perhaps even of the Church, who threatens excommunication, and a privation of holy burial: they are unwilling to appear to be what they really are, irregular in conduct, and devoid of religion: they are studious to preserve the good opinion of their wives, children, and friends, whilst in reality, their self-interest is their God, to which they prostitute all the powers of their soul: and therefore it generally follows, that those who habitually put off their communion to Easter, as they preserve their vicious habits, most commonly commit a sacrilege, because they are equally indifferent about religion and the Author of it.

Another says, I unfortunately fell into sin a month after my last communion, my religion, which inspires me with the greatest veneration for the sacrament, prevented my speedier approach, than at the following Easter.

The religious reverence which is here obtruded, is nothing more than positive ignorance. There can be no doubt, but that repentance should closely follow the sin, and communion repentance. Who in sound judgment, upon receiving a wound, delays sending for help, till months are expired? A third says: for years past I have not communicated; my religion has withheld me: the Eucharist is a most awful sacrament, and great is the preparation requisite to receive it: my veneration is too great, not to dread an abuse: it is better to refrain than communicate unworthily.

There is here much fallacy and hypocrisy, but no kind of reason or religion. One might as well say, it is better to die of hunger, than of poison:

it is better to live in mortal sin, than sin mortally: it is better to be damned for neglect of Easter duty, than be damned for an attempt to disgrace it: where on both sides of the question, there is only death, sin, and hell, nothing is better, or even good, all is bad, and bad in extreme. Between a sacrilegious communion, and no communion at Easter, there is the middle compound conduct, to communicate and communicate worthily. This alone can be the result of true religion, whilst an open violation of the law of Christ and of His Church, is a palpable breach of our essential obligation. I have known hundreds of hypocrites to affect a great fund of religion, and a particular respect for the Eucharist, by which they sometimes succeeded in imposing on the weak, and in obtaining the approbation of the ignorant: but were their religion real, and their respect genuine, their great care would be, to dispose themselves for, and not to shun the table of life. Their respect is for an idol of flesh, which they know not how to quit: it is for a criminal attachment, in which they are involved; for ill-gotten goods, which they are unwilling to restore; for a resentment, or a desire of revenge, which they harbor and foment; these obstacles must be removed before they can communicate worthily, and as they are unwilling to remove them, their sinful passions evidently have the preference over the love of their christian duty.

A fourth seemingly more candid and sincere, acknowledges himslf unworthy of communion, from a criminal habit unfortunately contracted: and because he retains a deep sense of religion, he refrains from a profanation of so great a sacrament. In this sort of language, there is a great abuse of terms: it is properly an extinction, and not a sense of religion, which withholds from communion a soul, who is thus miserably enthralled: for it is the very height of irreligion to prefer the object of our unruly passions to Jesus Christ, our God and Savior. There can be no religion or faith left in the man, who is impious enough to say, that he had rather be separated from his God, than from the object of his crime; and that he judges not his Savior worthy of the sacrifice of his pleasure, and of his sinful attachment. This determination of persisting in sin, rather than of taking any step to prepare for communion, is a preference most injurious to God, and a positive insult to His Divine Majesty. He who has come to this pass, most probably believes not in the real presence, or should he retain a spark of faith on that head, it resides on the lips, more than in the heart, as S. Paul expresses it, *they confess that they know God, but deny Him in their actions**.

True religion, in as much as it concerns the blessed Eucharist, is that, says the council of Trent, which engages and disposes us to receive it worthily and frequently, by sacrificing to this important purpose, every human consideration†. It is the religion which is exacted by our Redeemer: *unless you eat of the flesh of the son of man, you shall not have life in you.*

I now come to the objections which some zealous, but mistaken Christians, as vainly make to frequent communion, as the hypocritical sinner may do, to cloak his irreligion. The dignity, they say, and holiness of this sacrament is such, that four thousand years would be an inadequate space of time, to a suitable preparation for so holy an action: it should therefore seem, that the greater the interval is, between one communion and another, the better, and more worthy must the communicant be.

---

* Ep. ad Tit. i. 16.
† Omnes et singuli qui Christiano nomine censentur, hæc mysteria corporis et sanguinis dominici ea fide et constantia et firmitate credant . . . . ut frequenter suscipere possint. Trid. Sess. 13. c. 8.

S. Chrysostom however assures us, that the due disposition for communion, draws not its valuation from any space of time, but from purity of conscience. If the infinite dignity of the sacrament, be the direct and sole object of consideration, it will be readily granted, that no number of years can perfectly qualify us to receive it at any time: nevertheless, it is certain that those who communicate often, are in general better prepared, and more pleasing to God, than those who rarely correspond with the views of their divine Master. A piece of green wood frequently approached to the fire, will, by gradual evaporation of moisture, become fit to take fire: Jesus Christ is a burning flame of love, the oftener we visit Him, the more shall we be inflamed, by a gradual disincumbrance from earthly attachments. It is besides, a known truth, that one communion, is by far the holiest and the best preparation for another.

But does nor frequent communion insensibly lessen the respect which is due to this adorable sacrament? It is commonly said, that familiarity degenerates into contempt. This axiom holds good in relation to low and vulgar minds, who even without any near inspection, and at a distance, betray many weaknesses: but it is not so with great and virtuous souls, who grow on our esteem, from a better acquaintance with their good qualities. But even admitting that an intimacy with the most perfect man, should bring on indifference or disregard from the discovery of lurking blemishes, a familiarity with the God of heaven and earth, can admit of no such supposition: infinite is His grandeur, boundless is His majesty, numberless are His perfections, the nearer we view them, the more powerfully do they command our esteem, the more forcibly do they excite our love. A repitition of our visits to Him, as it brings on a new knowledge of that most ancient, yet ever recent bounty, inflames our love without lessening our respect: filial affection, and the greatest veneration are perfectly compatible with each other, and very admissible into the same breast. Frequent communion inspires a soul with the lowest and meanest sentiments of herself, and with the warmest and most respectful gratitude to the King of Glory, who deigns to admit her to His table: but this respect how great soever it may be redoubles her love, whilst her love alternately increases her respect for that God, who is at once great, and all bounteous. A frequent communicant besides, is endowed with more helps, than those who are remiss in this holy duty; he is therefore better able to pay all due attention to every motion of grace, and grace doubtless will teach him proper reverence and respect.

But it may be asked, whether a just and holy fear of the great majesty of God, should not withhold us from frequent communion, as it formerly withheld the Israelites from approaching to Mount Sinai? I answer that there is a fear which, originating from conscious guilt, causes us to fly from His formidable presence, and this fear is the result of sin, and seized our first parents on their transgression. "I heard your voice in paradise, and I feared you O Lord, and therefore I hid myself." Thus an unfaithful spouse dreads the presence of her husband; an undutiful child shuns his provoked parent: an awe like this is bad and prejudicial. There is another kind of fear which is commendable and praise worthy, because it arises from an unwillingness of displeasing God, and an apprehension of incurring guilt in His sight: a fear like this has no tendency to withdraw us from the divine presence, but rather prompts us to enjoy it, the better to be screened from danger, by its powerful influence. That awe alone is salutary and desirable, which leads and excites us to frequent communion. It is a folly, says Gerson, to abstain from communion through fear, while our conscience does not reproach us with mortal sin. The hope of meeting with succor, should be motive sufficient to engage us to go to Him, who alone can give us comfort. The law of Moses, that law of terror is now no more: we more fortunately live under the benign influence of the law of grace and of singular mercy. Our God, like a most bountiful father, invites His children to eat freely, familiarly, and frequently at His table: He demands, and certainly commands respect, but yet, is more jealous of our love and confidence. If our fear be rational, and such as becomes a Christian, it never will keep us from, but will spur us to communion: and when it has a contrary effect, our only fear should be, lest we incur the threats which our Lord has denounced against those tardy Christians, who refuse to partake of His grand supper.

A further query may occur: is frequent communion advisable to a Christian, whilst he feels no sensible devotion, no relish or desire of communion, and even labors under a degree of indolence and tepidity, and a crowd of involuntary distractions?

For a frequent participation of the divine mysteries, neither Jesus Christ or His Church, have ever exacted a sensible devotion; thousands of good and meritorious works are daily performed, independently of any perceptible relish or satisfaction: a sincere good will, an earnest desire of serving and pleasing God, is all He requires of us. Real and true devotion has no other constituents than a promptitude of will, an attention of mind, and a firmness of heart in the discharge of the duties incumbent upon us, in all which, nothing pleasing or naturally attracting need interfere. St. Bonaventure, Alger, and other holy doctors, clearly assert this doctrine: "Communicate notwithstanding this lifelessness and seeming tepidity, these distractions and involuntary dispositions; go and receive with confidence in God's mercy."* This state of reluctance, as it is unpleasant to self-love, serves only to increase in us self-abasement, and further to strengthen and confirm us in virtue.

The objection made to frequent communion taken from the consideration of our many faults and imperfections, is clearly answered and removed

---

* Si quandoque tepide, temen confidens de misericordia Dei fiducialiter accedat; nec ideo praetermittende est communio, si quandoque homo non sentit specialem devotionis gratiam cum ad illam se studet praeparare. Bonav. 1. de processu Rel. 7. proces. c.2.

by Gerson in the following manner: "He who refrains from communion because he is tepid and cold, resembles the man who should say, I keep from the fire because I am cold, and because I am sick I will have no physician: whereas the sick only require a physician, and such only as are cold, stand in need of warmth from the fire: the sacraments are medical, wherefore your infirmity has the greater occasion for them: Christ is a burning fire, if free from mortal sin, confidently approach Him, He will kindle your heart into love."*

"Eat confidently, says St. Augustine,† of this heavenly bread, bring to the altar a well intentioned mind, and although your sins may be daily, if they be not mortal, you have every reason to hope that the Eucharist will be an excellent food to you, and no poison."

There are others who conclude, that their communions must be useless and unprofitable, because they discover no progress they make in virtue, and their transgressions, though only venial, are daily the same."‡ St. Ambrose solves this difficul-

---

* Qui ad hoc sacramentum non accedit quia tepidus est ac frigidus, similis, est ei qui diceret: ad ignem non accedo quia frigidus sum, Medicum non requiro, quia infirmus sum. Sacramenta medicinæ sunt, etiamsi infirmus sis, accede. Christus ignis est, etiamsi frigidus sis, dummodo in peccato mortali non sis, accede. Gerson de præpar. ad Missam. † S. Aug. Tract. 26. in Joan. ‡ L. 4. de Sacram. c, 6.

ty, where he says: "Because I sin CONTINUALLY, I CONTINUALLY stand in need of the eucharistic medicine." And the council of Trent teaches, "That our Lord instituted this heavenly nourishment as a DAILY antidote against our DAILY infirmities and faults." *Sumi voluit ut antidotum, quo liberemur a culpis quotidianis.* Frequent communion therefore is not to be laid aside, nor to be supposed unprofitable, because our imperfections are daily: where communion is unfrequent, there are equally imperfections, and daily too, nay, in a greater number, and generally of a more serious nature. From the want of this daily food human weakness increases, and the sins which consequently are occasioned by it, are by far more alarming, than those which a frequent communicant complains of. Repeated communion is a lasting preservative against mortal sin; and this consideration alone, is proof enough of the expediency, and even necessity of it: it also keeps us in the fear and in the love of God, and at each time, imparts fresh courage to subdue our restless passions. Should our proficiency be imperceptible to us, as long as we are not conscious of a notorious neglect on our side, we should still preserve our peace of mind, by a patient acquiescence to the will of God: in heaven, I trust, we shall experience, that each one of our communions has purchased us a new crown, and additional degrees of felicity and glory: till we reach those mansions of bliss, let us rely on the goodness of God, and form our conduct on the dictates of faith. The greatest saints were unacquainted with the progress they made in virtue: nay, as they grew in perfection, they fell in their own valuation.

But some will say, are not our daily faults, and the many temptations and distractions we are subject to, sufficient proofs, that we are not in the grace of God, or at least, that we are not duly prepared for communion?

This question has amply been answered elsewhere; yet to remove, as much as possible, every vain fear and groundless apprehension from timorous souls, I think proper to repeat, that the state of grace, and the most perfect love, are perfectly compatible with those disagreeable concomitants of our nature. The saints themselves were not free from them; but to them, they were cogent motives of an habitual humiliation, on the one hand, whilst on the other, they induced them to frequent communion, as to the very best of remedies. A golden vase, ceases not to be gold because it is somewhat tarnished or dusty. If you communicate often, the gold of charity will soon brighten in you, and the dust of your daily failings will insensibly disappear.

It still may be urged, that several, who communicate frequently and even daily, are more irregular in conduct, than many others who communicate well, but seldom.

To avoid sophism, the comparison should run between those who communicate well, and often, and those who communicate well, and seldom. Thus is the argument fairly stated: and I assert, that reason, authority and experience clearly demonstrate, that the former are more virtuous, and receive more graces than the latter. I also advance on the same foundation, that those who rarely communicate, will find it no easy task to persevere, for any length of time, in the state of grace: whilst those who make the Eucharist their daily bread, and receive it worthily, move in a virtuous course with facility and pleasure.

If we compare those who communicate ill, and often, with those who communicate ill, and seldom, the latter, doubtless are less criminal; but, praise be to God, I exhort no one to anything so enormous, as one bad communion. Who is ignorant, that a sacrilegious abuse of this kind, is a treason of the blackest dye, a most injurious contempt of, and a most horrible insult offered to this adorable sacrament? This topic is the proper and necessary theme for the pulpit, but falls wide of my present purpose.

I could however wish to proclaim to all the world, and in particular to the greatest sinners, that they grossly err, and greatly injure the all bounteous providence of their Maker, as often as they despair of a reform of life, whilst they have it in their power to prepare themselves duly for communion: great, wonderful, inexpressible is the efficacy which flows from it on a contrite heart; in as much, as one only communion has power and virtue enough to change the greatest sinner into an eminent saint.

As to the notion of those who rarely communicate on account of their unworthiness, it will not stand scrutiny and close examination. For if they style themselves unworthy, from the infinite disproportion, which essentially subsists between the creator and the creature, in this light, nothing more is exacted than that we should communicate with a proper sense of our total dependence on our Maker. The Mother of God was not free from this sort of unworthiness, as it is inseperable from the idea of a creature: this purest however of all creatures was the object of God's great complacency, and, no doubt, set the example to the primitive Christians of daily communion. Or they style themselves unworthy, because their love of God, is yet unpurified and mixed with imperfections; but this kind of unworthiness is also inseparable from human nature, it only should be, when we communicate, an additional cause of humiliation, and never a reason for not communicating: could this deficiency authorize our forbearance, the angels alone could be duly qualified for the sacrament, which assertion positively clashes with the doctrine of the Church. Mortal sin is, absolutely speaking, that unworthiness alone, which should withhold Christians from communion: while they are free from that, they unreasonably abstain from this necessary food. The opinion of St. Cyril is no less instructive than it should be alarming to all such reasoners: "It is proper to inform those who have been baptized and have received the grace of God, that, if they refuse to receive Jesus Christ in the holy mysteries, on account of a feigned religion, they exclude themselves from life everlasting:" And this their refusal, though it seems to take rise from a fund of religion, in reality is scandalous and fraught with the greatest danger. There are two capital points, which all those who are in the state of grace, should invariably attend to and practice: let them, with great confidence, communicate very often: let them communicate with an earnest desire of a daily amendment of life: and while they wish to correct their daily delinquencies, they should reflect, that for this purpose, there are no means so efficacious as frequent communion.

CHAPTER XVI.

NO STATE OR CONDITION OF LIFE CAN PLEAD EXEMPTION FROM FREQUENT COMMUNION.

Having hitherto shown the insufficiency of some personal obstacles to frequent communion, I now come to the refutation of such objections as arise from the various departments of life, in which we are respestively placed; none of which, I maintain, can afford excuse sufficient for frequent communion.

When our Lord promised to give us His flesh to eat, as the master-piece of all His wonders, they were the Jews, who had assembled around Him, to whom He made this gracious promise, and as some of them from the hardness of the proposal, withdrew themselves from the crowd, instead of mitigating His first assertion, He emphatically declared to them all, "Unless you eat of my flesh, you shall not have life in you." Every Christian therefore, without distinction of state or condition, ought frequently to communicate. In the parable of the feast, among those who were invited to it, one alleged for excuse, a pair of oxen which he had to break in, another a country house which he had just bought, and the third, the marriage state he was newly engaged in; but the Master of the feast rejecting their excuses, threatened them with an absolute exclusion from His table in future, or, in other words, from the kingdom of heaven.

The apostles indiscriminately, as to state or position in life, gave daily communion to all the faithful. Poor and rich, women and men, old and young, partook of this heavenly food; and the Church in every age, has constantly invited all Christians in general, and every one in particular to the same refreshing table. "*Let all and every one among Christians . . . . believe with so lively

---

* Trid. Sess. 13. c. 2.

and so firm a faith, as to become worthy of FRE-QUENTLY receiving these holy mysteries."

As to those who are vested with the sacerdotal character, their obligation of frequent celebration, seems obvious and incontrovertible: the words, *do this in remembrance of me,* clearly show it, and express a divine precept which the apostle makes mention of, and enforces, when he says, "As often as you eat of this bread and drink of this cup, you shall announce the death of our Lord, until He comes to judge the world." Jesus Christ therefore, and the apostle in His name, commands all priests constantly and uninterruptedly to offer up the sacrifice of the mass to the day of judgment: *mortem Domini annunciabitis donec veniat:* and the council of Trent declares, that the Catholic Church has ever understood and taught it in this light*.

This duty of frequent celebration, is grounded also on the exalted dignity of every priest, who is through his priesthood the minister of God, of Jesus Christ and of His Church, the dispensator of His holy mysteries, and the mediator between man and his Maker. As God's minister, he is incessant-

---

* Ut offerrent præcepit per hæc verba; hoc facite in meam commemmorationem; uti semper ecclesia catholica intellexit et docuit.

ly to promote His greater honor and glory by those means which are most conducive to the end, and nothing surely is so glorifying, as the immolation of a divine victim. As minister of Jesus Christ, he is continually to renew the death of this God-man, after an unbloody manner, and thus perpetuate among the faithful, the remembrance of the prodigy of His love for man. As minister of the Church, he should studiously promote her interest, consult her welfare, and by his unrelenting piety, add daily to her lustre. As dispensator of God's holy mysteries, it is incumbent on him to distribute them to the faithful, according to their wants and exigencies: and finally as an intercessor for man who sins daily, daily, or at least frequent should be his offerings of propitiation, which, through the merits of Christ, procures pardon and forgiveness.

A good deal more might be said on this sacerdotal obligation, but having no reason to think that these pages will fall into the hands of any one who is not sufficiently instructed in the duties annexed to his vocation, I shall conclude on this head with the opinion of S. Bonaventure*.

---

* D. Bonav. de Præpar. Missæ.

"A priest in the state of grace, who neglects the celebration of mass, as far as in him lies, deprives the Blessed Trinity of the greatest glory, the angels of the greatest joy, sinners of the remission of their sins, the righteous of grace, the suffering souls of a mitigation of their pains, the Church of a singular blessing; he deprives himself of the best remedy for his daily failings, of an increase of grace, of a more ample forgiveness of his imperfections, of an abatement of concupiscence, of additional illustrations, of peace and content of mind, of further union with God, and of a greater help to the practice of every virtue."

Frequent communion is not less obligatory to religious people: and if some among the various orders which beautifully adorn the Church of God, have not daily communion enjoined them by rule, it is nevertheless, what is universally counselled and generally practiced in all religious orders of men, those who are in orders, sacrifice every morning: and there are communities of women, especially of the visitation of the blessed sacrament, in which several of every convent communicate daily. And if, to avoid too great a restraint, daily communion is not in general, of strict rule and command, there is also no rule which forbids it. When Jesus Christ and His Church exhort all the faithful to frequent communion, it should seem most rational to suppose, that religious people were more particularly spoken to, as their state of life is more peculiarly adapted to a strict union with God. The daily observance of their vows, their assiduity in prayer, in the recital of the divine office, their silence, recollection and self-denial, contribute to form a preparation for communion, far superior to what is within the reach of the laity. They abandon all, to possess Jesus Christ, and by what means can they possess Him, but by receiving Him in His sacrament. By frequent and daily communion, they bring back, and renew the fervor of primitive times: like the chosen people, God, in His mercy, has drawn them from the land of Egypt: He sends them a bread more heavenly than the manna, which they are to gather and feed upon daily, and it is this choicest of blessings, which chiefly constitutes the singular happiness of a religious state.

But the comforts accruing from this divine manna, are no ways confined to the cloister and convent. Those who live in the wide world, are equally invited to this heavenly banquet, and the obligation they are under of accepting the invitation, is, in one sense, greater than that of religious people, who are furnished with more means for salvation, whilst they are less exposed to temptation and danger.

There are two classes of people in life, married and unmarried: both the one and the other stand in need of frequent communion. The latter are encompassed by many perilous snares, which frequently prove too fatal without this heavenly support: and as to the marriage state, which was first instituted by the Almighty, and since, has been raised to the dignity of a sacrament, it can be no obstacle to frequent communion. The primitive Christians, as S. Francis of Sales observes, although married, communicate daily; and the Church of Christ has at no time excluded married people from frequent and even daily communion. On the contrary, we have elsewhere observed, that Pope Innocent XI. positively forbids all bishops, pastors and directors to refuse even daily communion to merchants and married people, provided that they are in the state of grace, and in earnest in the business of salvation: whatever else may be said or read on this particular, is a mere matter of counsel.

Neither are the distractions, hurries and avocations, which generally are inseperable from a family and from business, a sufficient obstacle to frequent communion: the following anecdote, relating to Sir Thomas More, lord chancellor of England, will elucidate what I mean. Several bishops, whose faith and morals were on the decline, loudly exclaimed against the custom he had entered upon, of communicating daily, alleging that a layman immersed, as he was, in a multiplicity of worldly affairs, should show more respect to the dignity of so great a sacrament. To which his reply was: "The very reasons which you bring to withdraw me from frequent communion, are exactly those which induce me to it: my dissipations are great and many; and communion brings on recollection; the occasions of offending God present themselves daily, and I daily arm myself against them by communion: I stand in need of wisdom and penetration to unravel, and conduct with propriety and justice, several intricate and perplexing matters, I therefore, every day, go and consult Jesus Christ in His holy sacrament."

It was through the efficacious influence of this great sacrament, that the primitive Christians were holy merchants and mechanics, faithful wives and husbands, trusty servants, and dutiful children, edifying parents, and disinterested arbitrators:

from the same source of grace, the wealthy in those days were charitable to their distressed neighbors; moderate in the midst of affluence, reserved and abstemious amidst the allurements of pleasure. The poor were content with their lot, and, in their poverty, they willingly resembled their indigent Master.

The afflicted also and the distressed, the sorrowful and unfortunate in life, more than most others, stand frequently in need of this sovereign remedy. The presence of their Savior will allay the storm, will lighten their burden, soothe their affliction, dispel all darkness, and strengthen them in battle: it is chiefly in distress that communion is necessary. It was so foretold by the royal prophet. "*Thou hast prepared for me a table of refreshment, to enable me to oppose those who molest me." This God of bounty, will dry up our tears, and enable us to bear up with suffering and affliction, if not immediately with joy, at least with patience and resignation.

On the other hand, the prosperous and the affluent, the great and dignified Christians are equally under a necessity of making frequent application to this great channel of grace. The

---

* Psalm xxii.

many snares with which they are surrounded, the various temptations which strongly allure them to forget themselves and the Author of their existence, will, if duly considered, constitute something beyond a counsel, not to say a strict obligation to frequent communion, at least in some certain circumstances, which often attend an elevated and wealthy station.

There is, I know, another class of people, who, free from vice, and inclined to virtue, could wish often to communicate, but are kept back by a latent dread of incurring blame and censure: they see the propriety as well as the advantage of this holy practice; but they are unwilling to appear singular, some even apprehend giving scandal. This is a snare which has been, actually is, and, I fear, will continue to be extremely prejudicial to thousands. The singularity which is here apprehended, purely originates from a decay of faith and of christian fervor. In former times, it would have been a singularity, and even a scandal, not to have communicated often; although you may therefore be singular in the eyes of the present age, by frequently communicating, you only walk in the steps of your ferverous forefathers: which practice of the two, is the most eligible? besides, where is the singularity, when you only avail yourself of your own right? Every son has a right to sit at his father's table: the sick only have occasion for a physician. If you be regular in conduct, and attentive to the discharge of the duties annexed to your state, you may possibly give an imaginary, but no real scandal. Should you be upbraided with your daily failings, S. Francis of Sales, bids you reply, that you communicate often, because you are imperfect, in hopes, through this excellent remedy, of daily growing better.

CHAPTER XVII.

OF THE HOLINESS OF COUNSEL RELATIVE TO FREQUENT COMMUNION.

We have already examined that kind of purity of heart, which we are commanded to possess before we can venture to communicate without profanation; we now come to that holiness of counsel, or of that perfection and sanctity of manners, which, though not of positive precept, is ever earnestly inculcated to all who aspire to frequent communion; the discussion of which, will throw a satisfactory light on the whole subject we have in hand. That we may proceed on safe and sure ground, the council of Trent shall direct our steps, and lay open to us, in the clearest point of view, the real meaning of Jesus Christ and of His Church, concerning the disposition which becomes frequent communion. The oracle is as follows: "That all and every one of the faithful, from a remembrance of the infinite grandeur, and of the extreme love of Jesus Christ who gives us His flesh to eat, may believe and reverence these holy mysteries with such DE-VOTION, that they may FREQUENTLY receive this bread which is above all substance." From whence it obviously appears, that the devotion which is here spoken of, is the result of a lively faith concerning the grandeur and infinite love of our Redeemer, and that this faith should powerfully induce us to frequent communion.

Now the character and the essential constituent of devotion in general, is, in the opinion of St. Francis of Sales, an ardent affection of the soul, which bends her to a ready compliance with the will of God, and is styled the flame of charity. In our present disposition, devotion is a fervorous inclination of a righteous soul towards the blessed Eucharist, which renders her serious and steady in a desire of, in a preparation for, and in an assiduity in frequent communion.

It is an affection of the soul, and not of the imagination or of the senses: it is therefore no ways incompatible with a crowd of distractions and temptations, nor yet with an involuntary tepidity, reluctance and disgust: and as the point of perfection to which it may extend is undetermined and boundless, the degrees of this perfection are consequently numberless. Some Christians attain many degrees of it, and others but few; communion, however, is fruitful and beneficial in proportion as this affection of the soul is active and ferverous. There is an habitual, and an actual devotion.

The habitual, is that which nourishes a warm desire of frequent communion, as being our sovereign good, our only treasure, the best remedy for every evil, and the best means to live in Jesus Christ. This pious inclination produces daily greater purity of heart, from the habitual desire of becoming more worthy of the possession of a God, and includes a fixed resolution of frequently partaking of this heavenly banquet, not vaguely and in general, but determinately at regular and stated times, so as to leave no room for chance, custom, humor or caprice. An indetermined desire of communicating often, as it does not deserve the appellation of a real desire, will also be productive of no great advantage. But the Christian who resolves to communicate on stated days in the month, or week, will reap infinite benefit from his holy resolution, because it will bring on great purity of conscience, and, will arm him with irresistable strength, against his enemies.

It is clear that this habitual desire of being united to Jesus Christ, will readily engage us in a faithful obedience to whatever He and His Church demands of us, and therefore daily communion will be the object of our warmest wishes: for as our faults and imperfections are daily, what can be more obvious than to wish for, and to apply a daily remedy?

Should this assertion seem too general, or impracticable to some Christians, a retrospect on the golden age of Christianity, will solve the difficulty. A larger share of faith, a greater regularity in conduct and manners, would wonderfully multiply communions amongst us, and bring Christendom back to that flourishing state, which was first established by Apostolic labor. We serve the same God, and profess the same faith, why should our conduct clash with their example?

Every motive induces me to avoid singularity in opinion, especially in religious matters: I therefore shall advance nothing of my own, when I come to determine how frequently Christians in general ought to communicate. The following are the most common rules which the Saints and Doctors of the Church have handed down to us; the inspection of them will diffuse a light over this important subject, the rays of which, many Christians stand greatly in need of, to discover the impropriety of the custom they have taken up, of going to the Sacrament but at indulgence times.

To be really serious in the business of salvation, monthly communion, in the estimation of S. Charles Boromeus, not only is expedient but even necessary: this monthly duty, our saint chiefly extends to those whose way of life is the most exposed to ignorance and dissipation, such as peasants, hard working people and soldiers; he is not however for excluding any of these denominations, from a more frequent participation of the holy mysteries, where the prevailing ignorance and dissipation of their state, can by any means be removed, and when their own inclination leads them to greater piety. But communion once a fortnight, is yet more advisable, because it better secures the only important affair. No practice whatever can so well shield us from sin, and from the many occasions which lead to it: and those who would advance in virtue and perfection, those who value a lasting repentance, and wish to keep up their fervor in the service of God, should communicate on every Sunday and holyday.

There are many who receive great favors from above, many who have great and interesting duties to discharge, many lead a regular and exemplary life, and are in earnest in the desire of salvation; all such will not exceed proper bounds, if they communicate four or five times a week, and even daily, especially within the Octaves of Easter, Whitsuntide, Christmas, Corpus Christi, and of the festivals of the Blessed Virgin: a devotion like this, will best impress on our minds a proper sense of those great mysteries, and will best benefit us unto life everlasting.

S. Charles exhorts us to communion before we go upon a journey, or undertake an affair of consequence: when we have been successful in our undertakings, when we recover from sickness or escape from danger: he advises the same practice, as often as God is pleased to visit us with affliction and adversity: when a parent, child, or friend is taken from us; when we wish for the conversion of any of our friends: on the anniversary of our baptism; on the feast of the saint whose name we bear, &c.

S. Charles, S. Francis, de Sales and Maldonatus, are for frequent communion among young people, particularly among students and cardinal Toletus determines that, when weekly, it generally is the most expedient and salutary. The opinion of S. Thomas is, that when youth are come to be susceptible of devotion, they are to be admitted to the sacred table. What favorable judgment therefore can be formed of such parents and pastors, as keep form communion those intrusted to their care, till they have got up to the age of sixteen or seventeen, and perhaps twenty years? Are they first to forfeit their baptismal innocence, and become almost incorrigible, before they are to partake of this heavenly food? Frequent communion is the best preservative against vice, the best support to virtue, and is more necessary to a Christian at that critical and slippery period of life, than at any other. The same saints and doctors, the rituals of many dioceses, and several provincial conucils advise also frequent communion in time of sickness, especially to those who, when in health, were used to that holy custom.

Actual devotion, which is much recommended to frequent communicants, is an ardor of soul which rouses and collects together the powers of mind and heart, for the better reception of so great a guest: before communion it excites lively sentiments of confidence, love, and such like virtues, and after communion, it produces similar sentiments of amorous thanksgivings, and engages the soul to relish the sweetness of the presence of her spouse, and quietly to listen to his interior voice.

And here I wish to observe, that the anxiety and solicitude which some carry with them to communion, is greatly hurtful to actual devotion. The God whom we receive, is a God of peace and tranquillity, and it is His delight to dwell in a peaceable heart. He indeed is the source of this peace, and He brings it with Him: our exterior and interior should savor of nothing but of joy and of confidence. He speaks to us, as He did to His apostles, "Fear not, peace be with you, it is I, who am your God and Savior."

All fear and anxiety which intervene at communion, are occasioned by the malice of our ghostly enemy, who at that time, more than at any other, labors to distress and annoy us. He suggests to some, the magnitude of their former transgressions, the uncertainty of their being forgiven, and consequently the danger of a sacrilege: to others he magnifies their daily failings, and tempts them to an endless discovery of hidden commissions, by which wile, several are piteously deluded, and scrupulously tormented. Whereas a rational and prudent discussion and examination of our interior on the one hand, joined to a due sorrow and purpose of amendment on the other, should be motive enough to compose us in peace, especially when we reflect that it is no tyrant, but a most indulgent father we give the meeting to. For all such perplexities however, no remedy is so efficacious, as proper obedience to a prudent director.

While some tire and fatigue themselves in endeavors to bring on a more sensible devotion, there are others who are pained by fruitless attempts, to remove involuntary distractions, which naturally redouble from the very solicitude they engage in. No good can ever arise from an agitated mind: calmness alone can prove beneficial. When you feel a want of devotion, when you find that you wander involuntarily from your purpose, bring gently to mind the motives which should make you fervorous, and calmly bring back your thoughts to the object on which you wish to fix them. That nicety and precision of comportment which some, on this occasion are restless in aiming at, are more the effect of a lurking pride, than of true devotion: their chief desire is to be satisfied with themselves, without paying much attention to the easy terms on which God is satisfied with them; whilst their intention is upright and pure they need no better preparation; to look for angelical perfection, in a mind weighed down by a mass of corruption, would be either folly or presumption. When we communicate, our whole attention should be given to our mighty and loving guest, to whom we should penitently, yet confidently acknowledged that we are truly objects of compassion, and therefore, the best entitled to mercy.

At that important moment, we should, like Magdalen, sit silent at His feet, and allow Him leisure to take possession of, and to speak to our hearts.

The husbandman in quiet expectation, abandons to the benign influence of the sun, the soil he has duly cultivated: and in proper season, his wishes are crowned with a plentiful harvest. Jesus

Christ, the sun of justice, would, in like manner, illuminate and warm us with His love, would sow, and bring forth in us the practice of every virtue, did not a certain activity and hastiness on our part, retard His divine influence: our constant prayer should be, "Speak, O Lord, for thy servant heareth."

Neither is the same degree of devotion expected from every one. Our God, who is goodness itself, is sufficiently pleased with that degree which is best suited to our present strength; and even though not quite free from some venial faults, or from an involuntary coldness and indifference, if we seek Him from our heart, He will make us welcome.

In this manner did king Ezechiah insist on the celebration of the paschal lamb, although a great part of the people had not been purified according to the rigor of the legal rites. He prayed to God in their behalf, and said: "Lord, thou art all-bounteous, and thou wilt pardon those who come to thee with their whole heart; thou wilt not impute to them as a sin, should they be less prepared than they ought to be." The Lord heard his prayer, and was propitious to his people.

Many are the methods which are pointed out to attain actual devotion: there are books without number on this subject, and every one should follow that method, which is best suited to his taste. For my part, I am of opinion, that, as our Lord chiefly instituted this sacrament to impress on our minds and hearts the memory of His mysteries and of His excessive love of man, most tender and inflamed would our devotion be, did we regularly reflect on these mysteries, as the Church successively celebrates them in the course of the year. In Advent, for instance, I am going to receive Jesus Christ my Lord and God, who, for my sake, became an infant, and was adored by the shepherds, the sages and the angels. In Lent: I am going to receive Jesus Christ my Savior, who sinks under the weight of my sins, who agonises and sweats blood, who is scourged, buffeted, crowned with thorns, and finally expires on a cross to give me life. At Easter: I am going to receive Jesus Christ my God, who being resuscitated, heals the sick, gives sight to the blind, awakens the dead, forgives sins, and instructs the apostles. By these, and such like considerations, the thought of our Lord would press strongly on our minds, and sink deeply into our hearts, which would constantly keep up in our breasts the flame of charity.

There are some, who, from a mistaken notion of decency and reverence, are reluctant to communicate two days together: this difficulty is vain and groundless. Our Redeemer, who most ardently desires to reign absolute over our hearts, not only for a day, but every moment of our life, cannot object to our love and confidence: neither can we suppose that the Christian, who is more holy from the grace he received in this day's communion, can be less worthy of communion to-morrow. The third day has the advantage over the second, and the fourth over the third, from the efficacy and virtue of the sacrament, which imparts to the soul worth and merit, proportionably as it is often and daily received. He, who, by means of the best acts of devotion, prepares himself for one communion, has doubtless an immediate right to another: now the grace which flows from the first, is superior in excellency to any other preparation and consequently paves the way for a second. We would allow of repeated and continued communions to one, whom we believed endowed with the gift of prophecy and of miracles: the advantage however of one communion is infinitely preferred to all such exterior gifts, which, in themselves, are no way connected with interior merit and virtue.

CHAPTER XVIII.

ON THE STRICT OBLIGATION OF FREQUENT COMMUNION.

There are some, so very ignorant of their Christian duties, that though they admit of the advantages arising from frequent communion, they no further consider communion in general, as incumbent upon them, than it is yearly enjoined by an ecclesiastical law. Whereas they ought to know that frequent communion, is as essential a duty, and as formal a command of our Lord and Master, as any proclaimed to us by holy writ. The words, *take ye and eat, do this in remembrance of me*, have invariably been understood and taught by the Church, as an express command, both of sacrifice and sacrament, incumbent on clergy and laity: for so we are informed by the council of Trent*. "Our Savior, says the said council, has instituted this sacrament, and has ORDERED that by nourishing ourselves with it, we should honor his memory, and announce his death till he comes to judge the world.†"

---

* Dominus Deus . . ut offerrent PRÆCEPIT: ut etiam ecclesia catholica semper intellexit et docuit. Trid. Sess. 22. c. 1.

† Salvator noster sacramentum hoc instituit, et in illius sumptione colere nos sui memoriam PRÆCEPIT, et annunciare mortem donec ipse ad judicandum mundum veniat. Sess. 13. c. 2.

When He says, *take ye and eat, do this in remembrance of me,* He at once commands the oblation, the consecration, the communion of the priest, and the distribution of the Eucharist to the faithful. For He commands His apostles and their successors to do in future what He then did. He then distributed the Eucharist, they therefore must do the same to the end of the world. This precept is still more clearly specified, where we read, "Verily, verily I say unto you, unless you eat of the flesh of the son of man, you shall not have life in you."

It is allowed, that, certain as it may be, that there is such a precept, it is no where determined what number of communions in the month or year we are strictly obliged to: but if we reflect on the motive for which this law was given, and on the purpose for which the blessed Eucharist was instituted, we readily shall discover our determinate obligation: this gracious purpose says the council of Trent, is spiritually to feed our souls, to free us from venial commissions, and to guard us against greater excesses: as often therefore as communion is necessary to preserve us in grace, and to shield us from grievous transgressions, so often is communion strictly binding and of divine precept. This is the unanimous opinion of the fathers, doctors, and councils.

Communion then is commanded as a help, morally necessary to save ourselves, as a help, the best calculated for that purpose, nay, and to several, as the only means of salvation. Prayer, fasting, bodily austerity, alms-deeds, and solitude, are, indeed, powerful means to secure eternal life; but labor, or bad health, incapacitate several from mortification and fasting; a multipliciy of affairs and avocations, preclude assiduity in prayer; many are unable to show their charity; retirement is incompatible with a family and business: but frequent communion is within every one's reach, it will powerfully protect us from danger, and preserve us in life and in health. Without this help, many among the faithful will labor in vain to subdue their passions, and to conquer their ghostly enemies. If in the many conflicts they are engaged in, they wish to come off victorious, they will find it necessary that God should frequently reign in their heart. Very sinful therefore must their neglect be, as often as they omit to avail themselves of a remedy, at once so ready and powerful against every evil. In this sense,

S. Francis of Sales writes, "*That those unfortunate Christians, who perish in eternity, will be destitute of every plea, when they stand before their Judge, who will convince them that they wantonly ran on to death, whilst, by means of this heavenly support, they might have preserved their lives: foolish people, he will say, why did you die, at the time you had at command this life-giving food?"

So necessary is frequent communion to continue in grace, that experience has shown, that many who have omitted this duty longer than they were prudently advised to abstain from it, have fallen into sin immediately on their neglect; for though we are promised help to avoid every snare, it is only upon condition that we slight not the means, we have at hand, of coming off victorious. S. Augustine must have considered frequent communion in this light, when he styled it a christian duty. He remarkably elucidates the point in question. "To you who have been newly christened, I had promised to give you a discourse on the sacrament of the Lord's table, which you now behold, and of which yesterday you partook: it is

---

* Devout Life, 2. p. c. 20.

incumbent on you to know what it is that you have received, what you are to continue to receive, and what you are in duty bound to receive DAILY: that bread which you see on the altar, being consecrated by the word of God, is the body of Christ."*

To the above testimony, I could add many more of the ablest divines, but not to be prolix, I confine myself to that of the learned and greatly admired Tourneli, who asserts, "That all the faithful are bound by divine precept, to preserve the life of their soul, for which happy preservation this sacrament was instituted by our Lord. . . I maintain that the faithful are strictly obliged FREQUENTLY to receive the Eucharist." †

The ecclesiastical law, concerning communion, obliges but once in a twelve-month, but besides this law, there exists another, which is from Christ,

---

* Promiseram vobis, qui baptizati estis sermonem, quo exponerem mensæ Dominicæ sacramentum, quod modo etiam videtis, cujus nocte præterita participes facti estis; debetis scire quid accepistis, quid accepturi estis, quid QUOTIDIE accipere debeatis. Panis ille, quem videtis in altari, sanctificatus per verbum Dei, corpus est Christi. Aug. serm. 227. ad recens baptiz.

† Tenentur omnes fideles jure divino studere conservationi vitæ spiritualis, et hoc sacramentum institutum est a Christo ad conservationem hujus vitæ. *Et infra.* Respondeo. debere fideles FREQUENTER ad sacram Eucharistiam accedere. L. de Sacram. Euch. art. 3.

and imports frequent communion: this the Church can neither alter or restrain. And, indeed, it has always been the remotest from her views to attempt either: on the contrary, in every age, she has constantly taught, and, as much as possible, has strongly enforced, both to clergy and laity, frequent, and even daily communion. In the first ages, she excluded from the benefit of her prayers and sacrifices, those who did not communicate daily: in process of time, she restrained her censures to a weekly neglect; in later periods, as fervor decreased with the increase of her members, she limited her punishment to three times in a year, Christmas, Easter, and Whitsuntide. Finally, she has judged it prudent to confine excommunication to the neglect of Easter only. He therefore, who at present, only communicates at Easter, evades, it is true, ecclesiastical censure; but does not, by that communion, fulfil the divine law, which enjoins frequent communion. For, besides the penal law which is annexed to a neglect of Easter duty, there is a directive precept of more frequent communion, which is virtually contained in the ampliative expression; *at least:* the real meaning of which is, you shall communicate at Easter, and at other times, as often as it shall be necessary to enable you to avoid sin, and persevere in grace: if at Easter you are deficient in that duty, you shall incur ecclesiastical censure: and as to those other communions which you stand in need of for salvation, and which you abstain from, the Church leaves them to God's just judgment.

We have observed, that neither the divine, or the ecclesiastical precept, determinately point out any number of communions throughout the year. Which specified number is wisely omitted, because it would not be practicable, nor yet expedient that all should be guided by the same rule. The various dispositions, characters, exigencies, and conditions induce relative obligations on some, which others, in dissimilar circumstances, may not be immediately subject to. We have all, however, an invariable and certain rule to conduct ourselves by, in the following words: *He who eats of my flesh shall never die.* We are therefore to regulate our communions according to our wants; if these be many and great, those should be proportionably frequent; for as grace is constantly to be preserved, and sin at all times to be avoided, so at all times are proper means to bo used, to preserve the one, and to avoid the other.

A neglect of frequent communion, is not only a violation of the law of Jesus Christ, but also a considerable breach of well regulated charity, which obliges every one, to consult, after the best manner he can, one's real interest and happiness, for which purpose, frequent communion is the very best means. Greatly therefore inimical must he be to himself, and strangely inattentive to his greatest concerns, who by so gross a neglect, exposes himself to the danger of forfeiting the favor of God. The man who, in the midst of plenty, should die through hunger, from an obstinate refusal of nourishment, would be guilty of suicide: a refusal of this heavenly support is proportionably the more criminal, as the life of the soul is superior to a temporal existence.

This same neglect is a criminal contempt of the law of Christ, who not only invites to, but also commands frequent communion. For if we penetrate into the hearts of those who rarely communicate, the real reason will be found to be, that they prefer the creature to the Creator, and an indulgence of their passions, to christian sobriety and self-denial. Ingratitude also is joined to contempt: the God whom we adore in the Eucharist ardently wishes to live within us, and habitually to reign over us, with all the charms of his bounty, and all the treasures of His Divinity; to compass this great end, he overthrows, by a crowd of prodigies, the established laws of nature. The revelations, visions and raptures, with which He has at times gifted many of His faithful servants, are not comparable to the value and advantage of one communion: this inestimable blessing is daily at our option; but alas! how few avail themselves of their invaluable privilege! Most make little or no account of the bliss which the angels could wish to taste. Jesus Christ resides in our tabernacles, *in mundo erat,* whilst we affect not to know Him : *et mundus eum non cognovit:* He claims a dominion over our hearts, as his own property : *in propria venit,* and we His inheritance and His children, refuse Him admittance into our breasts, *et sui eum non receperunt.* What is injustice, what is ingratitude, if this be not the greatest?

But what, in one sense, is still more deplorable, a neglect of this kind is no ambiguous sign of final reprobation : "It is much to be feared," says S. Cyprian, "lest he who is long separated from the body of Jesus Christ, should also be very remote from eternal salvation *." And we read in the

---

* Serm. de Cæn. Dom.

council of Agatha, that, "Those among the laity who do not communicate at Christmas, Easter and Whitsuntide, are not be deemed Catholics *." As the happiness of the saints in heaven consists in the possession of Jesus Christ, so the misery the reprobate are plunged in, consists in their eternal separation from Him. Those who refused to possess Him in time, are not likely to enjoy Him in eternity: and while they flew from Him in His sacrament, they have little reason to hope that He will be their everlasting reward. Besides, what is generally the consequence of such a neglect? A train of irregularities and vices, which too readily lead to certain perdition.

But may it not be deemed a presumption to communicate often, as those who do so, must entertain no bad opinion of their own worth and merit? I answer, that there is no presumption in thinking one's self worthy of communion, that is, in thinking one's self in the state of grace, and in one's believing that he may often receive worthily. It is an incumbent duty on every Christian to be habitually averse to, and exempt from sin. And

---

* Sœculares, qui in natali Domini, Pascha. Pentecoste non communicaverint, Catholici non credantur, nec inter catholicos habeantur. Con. Agath. c. sœculares. de consec. dist. 2.

S. Augustine expressly says, "* That every one of the faithful, when in the state of grace, may say, I AM HOLY: when you acknowledge your own insufficiency, and proclaim the gift, you are not arrogant but grateful." It is not humility, but absurdity to fancy ourselves in the state of sin, if we have either lived regularly, or done penance for past offences. Religion and true piety are perfectly conformable to, and no ways inconsistent with common sense and reason.

But what seems to me to be the height of presumption is, to refrain from, to oppose, or disapprove of frequent communion, notwithstanding that it is enforced and commanded by the oracles of Jesus Christ, the decisions of His Church, and the practice of the saints in every age; thus, I say, to prefer one's private judgment to that of the author of our holy religion, to stand up, and make head against all antiquity, and the supreme tribunal of Christ's Church, is an intolerable obstinacy and a consummate arrogance. Some blame the conduct of such directors as enjoin frequent communion, by way of satisfaction, in the tribunal of

---

* Dicat unusquisque, fidelium SANCTUS sum: non est ista superbia elati, sed confessio non ingrati. Habere te agnosce, et ex te nihil habere, ut nec superbus sis, nec ingratus. Aug. in Psal. lxxxv.

penance: the censure however is improper, and can only be passed by those, who either are unwilling seriously to enter on a reform of life, or are avowed enemies to frequent communion. No injunction can be more interesting and salutary than this, as it is at once the most efficacious, and the most expeditious means both of conversion and perfection. He who is happy enough to meet with a guide, who leads him through this path, will soon be properly formed to the school of Christ, and presently will learn to triumph over himself, the world and the powers of darkness. This practice was familiar to the most zealous followers of the apostles, such as Saints Vincent Ferreri, Charles Borromeus, Francis Xavier, Francis of Sales; and the holy priest Eude, whose repute was great in the conversion of souls, in his excellent book on a good director, He recommends frequent communion as the best sacramental injunction.

CHAPTER XIX.

FREQUENT COMMUNION IS A FUNDAMENTAL POINT OF THE CHRISTIAN RELIGION.

Having proved that frequent communion is not barely an arbitrary devotion, but an incumbent duty on every Christian, my present endeavor is to show the importance of it, and how essential a connection it bears with revealed religion. As in other assertions, so also in this, the authority of the fathers, doctors, and councils, shall support and lead me on.

In the opinion of S. Thomas, the Eucharist is the sacrament of sacraments, the ultimate end for which they were instituted, it is the consummation of grace and of a spiritul life, and the helps and graces which flow from the other sacraments, are only suitable preparations for a worthy reception of this; a neglect therefore of this sacrament, is evidently a neglect of the fundamental part of religion: for which reason, S. Chrysostom remarks, as we have seen elsewhere, *That rare and

---

* Hom. in Ep. ad Tim.

unfrequent communion is what breeds every disturbance in the church of God."

The council of Reims says, "As the Christian religion does not contain any thing more valuable and more excellent than the sacrament of the Eucharist, nor yet any thing which is more conducive to a holy life, than a MOST FREQUENT participation of the holy sacrament, we greatly grieve that many among the Christians of our days, should be so neglectful as to receive it but once a year .... let pastors therefore use every endeavour to persuade the faithful, that there are no better or more compendious means, than most frequent communion, to extinguish heresies, and restore the church to her apostolical splendor *."

From hence it appears, that the council ascribes to unfrequent communion the rise and progress of all heresy, and to the contrary practice, a fair image of primitive lustre.

"Were you to deprive the church," says the learned Abbot Rupertus, "of the daily sacrifice,

---

* Cum nil habeat Christiana religio sacramento Eucharistæ præstantius, nilque ad sancte vivendum efficacius ejusdem sacramenti FREQUENTISSIMA participatione, dolemus tantam esse Christianorum hujusce temporis incuriam, ut semel tantum in anno sumant: . . . quare persuadere nitantur nullum effe modum aptiorem et compendiosiorem, quo sopitis et extinctis hæresibus ecclesiæ apostolicæ facies redeat. Concil. Rem. Act. 1.

which brings to our mind the funeral of our Lord, you would soon see with what propriety he might say, *what benefit arises from my blood?* For then the remembrance of Him, which, by means of this daily offering, now warms every breast, would presently be obliterated; charity would decay; faith would languish, hope would lose footing, and the loud cry of the blood of the righteous Abel, would no longer be heard, which cry is DAILY renewed in this great sacrifice, and daily opens the mouth of the Church, to take in so precious a draught *."

Suppress frequent communion, and you equivalently suppress the three theological virtues: doubts even concerning the real presence would ensue; vice and immorality would erect their standard, and assert their empire over the Christian world. The histories of latter times demonstrate the truth of my assertion.

What several nations and kingdoms have still reason to deplore, from a neglect of this life-giving

---

* Aufer a cœtu ecclesiæ quotidianas salvatoris nostri exequias, et vide quam merito dicat ipse salvator, *quæ utilitas in sanguine meo?* Refrigescente enim ea, quo hoc modo nunc ubique calet ejus memoria, refrigescet universa charitas, muta erit fides, claudicabit spes, conticescet magnus ille clamor sanguinis justi Abel, qui per traditum tanti sacrificii ritum, quotidie reparat vocem, quotidie laxat os bibentis et vociferantis terræ, scilicet ecclesiæ. Rupertus de Offic. Div. l. 2. c. 10.

food, is daily visible in particulars, who follow their unhappy example. For want of this nourishment, they relent in the practice of virtue, their religion becomes a burden, their languid faith holds but by a thread to the fold of Christ: nay, if in the long run they become not avowed apostates before men, they often are really so, in the sight of God.

On the contrary, by frequent communion, our faith, hope and charity quicken, and grow perfect; and as far as in us lies, we contribute to our Saviour's dominion throughout the world, according to the canticle of the Church: "Let us adore Christ our king, who by giving himself for their food, extends His empire over all nations *."

There can be no doubt but we are infinitely honored, as often as our Lord vouchsafes to admit us to His sacred table; but we also, on our part, honor and glorify Him by communion, in a manner the most exalted and the most worthy of a God; it is an act of supreme worship, and of the most transcendant pitch of adoration which man can pay Him: for it is nothing less than a God whom we offer to God, a God who jointly with us,

---

* Invi. Off. Fest. Cor. Christ.

and in us, adores and glorifies the supreme Being. It was no doubt for this reason, that Ignatius the martyr, styled the Eucharist the glory of our Lord; and * therefore was so pressing, that all should FREQUENTLY partake of it.

The Christian who often complies with this duty, gives the strongest proof of his belief in the words of his Master, and of his confidence in His infallible promises: and this steadiness of faith and of hope, reflects the highest degree of honor that man can return to the Deity. To believe that bread is changed into the body, and wine into the blood of Christ, that the same body is in many places at once, in heaven, in the Eucharist, and in millions of places upon earth; that the whole body of a perfect man is in the smallest particle that can be discerned, and all this in opposition to the relation of our senses, in opposition also to the efforts of Satan, the impetuosity of our passions, the force of bad example and of heterodox principles, is glorious to Christ who has revealed these truths, because He is firmly believed to be incapable of either deceiving or of being deceived.

---

* Festinate ergo FREQUNTER accedere ad Eucharistiam, id est, ad gloriam Domini. Ep. 14.

In the Eucharist, the miracles which our Saviour wrought during His mortal life are continually renewed. The dead then were brought to life, the blind saw, the sick were healed : here millions receive the life of their soul, the light of eternal truths guides their steps, all infirmities and diseases are removed, the devils of impurity, pride, sloth, envy, discord and dissension are put to flight : and the opposite virtues, by frequent communion, take root, and flourish in the Christian world.

Frequent communion is also a solemn renewal of our holy religion. To know Jesus Christ, His grandeur and mysteries is eternal life. The Eucharist is a lively exhibition of these mysteries, such as His incarnation, nativity, His death, resurrectio and miracles. The Christian who communicates on these festivals, renews those proper sentiments of virtue, which each of these great truths respectively must excite : he habitually lives in Christ, and Christ lives in him : and thus, by a sacramental union, anticipates the eternal fruition, which he has every motive to hope for.

Lastly, frequent communion is a strong proof of our holy religion, because it is a palpable accomplishment of several prophecies which foretold and asserted it. According to the royal prophet,

"There is to be a numerous church, composed of all nations, formed by the true Messiah, and they shall be styled the people of God*. The poor and the rich shall eat what they adore, and adore what they eat, by which they shall be satiated." And elsewhere, "the Lord in His great mercy and goodness, has renewed in a compendious manner, the remembrance of all His wonders, by giving food to those who fear Him †." This compendium of prodigies, is no other than the Eucharist, and those truly fear the Lord, who frequently receive it.

The prophet I say ‡, rapt into future time, beholds it pregnant with the Christian Church, founded on the top of a mountain, "On which the Lord will prepare for all the nations of the earth a most delicious banquet, where they shall drink a most exquisite wine, and death shall be thrown headlong into the abyss." The Eucharist is this con-

---

* Narrabo nomen tuum fratribus meis, in media ecclesiæ laudabo te . . . edent pauperes et saturabuntur . . . et adorabunt in conspectu ejus universæ familiæ gentium. Quoniam Domini est regnum, et ipse dominabitur gentium: manducaverunt et adoraverunt omnes pingues terræ . . . annuntiabunt cœli justitiam ejus: populo qui nascetur quem fecit Dominus. Psal. xxi.

† Psal. cx.

‡ Isaias xxv.

tinual feast which characterises the Christian religion, and precipitates into the abyss immorality and sin, which alone can give death to the soul.

The prophet Malachiah, speaking in the name of the Lord, reproaches the priests of the old law, with a neglect of proper worship, and threatens them with His vengeance: "* Unworthy ministers, from hence forward I reject your offerings ; your sacrifices shall cease, and your mode of worship shall be abolished: I behold a religion extending from east to west, which alone shall glorify the grandeur of my name: yes, from every corner of the globe, there is offered to me an unspotted victim, which completes my glory among all nations."

This pure and spotless oblation, which, at once, abolishes and supplies the places of all other sacrifices, which is become the only pleasing victim to the Most High, and which alone is to continue to honor Him as He deserves to be honored, is the adorable body and blood of Jesus Christ, who throughout the world, is daily immolated and eaten by numberless priests and fervent Christians, not only spiritually, but also by a real participation of the Eucharist, and therefore S. Chry-

---

* Malach. I.

sostom invites us to observe, "* How wonderfully and clearly the prophet explains the mysterious table of Christians, at which the unbloody victim is eaten."

Daniel † foretells that antichrist, to efface the memory of our Lord, and deprive mankind of the benefit of frequent communion, will abolish the sacrifice of the mass till then uninterrupted: as therefore the cessation of frequent communion is the proof of the existence of antichrist, the practice of it must necessarily prove the reign of Jesus Christ, and of the truth of his religion.

S. Paul commands a constant communion and offering, until the second coming of our Lord, that we may continually receive benefit from the mystery of our redemption: this precept is complied with by those priests who daily offer this unspotted Lamb, and by those among the faithful, who daily, or frequently communicate.

Our blessed Redeemer, on two different occasions, compares the kingdom of heaven, that is, His Church, to a great feast, to which all mankind are invited. It is truly a great feast, because the

---

* S. Chrys. hom. in Psalm xcv.
† Dan. viii. v. 11, 12. c. xii. v. 11.

meat and drink put before us, are His own flesh and blood. He who shall eat of this heavenly food, shall not die, but shall enjoy life everlasting: and he who refuses to partake of it, shall die the death of sin, and, shall be excluded from eternal life. He even expresses a desire of compulsion, *compelle intrare*, that no one may be destitute, and lost for want of this powerful help.

Such then are the oracles which, above three thousand years ago, spoke of the empire of a God over a people collected from all parts of the globe, who should honor and glorify His holy name by the unparalleled prodigy of the eucharistic sacrament. Nor is the accomplishment of them less marvellous than the prediction. The Messiah makes His appearance in the world, He forms the people He is to reign over, and commissions His disciples to disseminate His doctrine throughout the universe. They obey, and their obedience is successful: for near two thousand years past the nation of Christians, made up of all nations, has glorified God by the unbloody sacrifice of a Godman, which at once pays due honor to the Deity, and sanctifies man. In the days of the apostles, communion was daily. From their days to ours, the bishops, and their respective Churches, the doctors and their schools, the founders of religious orders, and their respective followers, the saints, in company with their disciples, the pastors at the head of their flocks, particular as well as general councils, the sovereign pontiffs, at the head of the universal Church, have unanimously persevered in the same doctrine, and invariably have continued to invite the faithful to a most frequent participation of this incomparable feast. Such is the glorious spectacle, which every age, from the apostles, exhibits to our view: what motives can be adduced, what reasons be alleged, why this holy practice should be superseded by the age we live in? A deviation from a point of doctrine, so essentially interwoven with the religion of Christ, as frequent communion has been proved to be, must evidently be erroneous and antichristian.

FINIS.

THE
CONTENTS OF THIS BOOK.

CHAPTER I. The pretended respect for the blessed Eucharist, which withdraws the faithful from frequent communion, is erroneous and dangerous.   Page 5

CHAP. II. The words of Jesus Christ, when he instituted the Eucharist, imply frequent communion.   14

CHAP. III. The actions of Jesus Christ, which relate to the Eucharist, imply the obligation of frequent communion.   30

CHAP. IV. The doctrine and practice of the apostles, and of the primitive Christians, prove the expediency of frequent communion.   43

CHAP. V. The doctrine and practice of the ancient Fathers of the Church, prove also the expediency of frequent communion.   53

CHAP. VI. The doctrine and practice of the leading scholastic doctors, concerning this subject.   71

CHAP. VII. Decisions of councils, both general and particular, on frequent communion.   86

CHAP. VIII. Decisions and regulations of Sovereign Pontiffs, through a succession of ages, concerning frequent communion.   97

CONTENTS.

CHAP. IX. The opinion and practice of the saints, concerning frequent communion. 113

CHAP. X. Of the holiness requisite and commanded for worthy and frequent communion. 140

CHAP. XI. The excellency of the holiness which is of precept. 154

CHAP. XII. The apostles and the Church of God, have at all times admitted to communion, those who possessed the holiness of precept. 167

CHAP. XIII. Frequent communion is the most powerful and efficacious help to salvation. 180

CHAP. XIV. Frequent communion is our greatest comfort and hoppiness in the way of salvation. 193

CHAP. XV. Frequent communion is vainly opposed by sinners as well as by some virtuous people. 202

CHAP. XVI. No state or condition of life can plead exemption from frequent communion. 220

CHAP. XVII. Of the holiness of counsel relative to frequent communion. 230

CHAP. XVIII. On the strict obligation of frequent communion. 243

CHAP. XIX. Frequent communion is a fundamental point of the Christian religion. 255

www.ingramcontent.com/pod-product-compliance
Lightning Source LLC
Chambersburg PA
CBHW032132230426
43672CB00011B/2314